Victory Lap

Fanniegate Recap & Release

G. Richard Bradford, III

Copyright © 2024 G. Richard Bradford, III

All rights reserved.
Written originally in English.

G. Richard Bradford III.

ISBN-13: 979-8301782206
Printed in the United States of America

THIS IS BECAUSE I CAN

9 8 7 6 5th I plead the

Jo Mamma's Edition

The Beginning of The End

It is November 27, 2024. Despite it being publicly reported at this point that the incoming Trump administration will effectuate recap and release next year the junior preferreds still trade at prices where you can make 2-3x your money in the next 12 months on recap and release.

The courts were worthless aside from making this a political trade. Obama stole Fannie and Freddie money to fund Obamacare. Biden didn't do anything even though he could have. Trump, in his first term, followed the law and started the retention of capital and got within 6 months of recap and release except COVID-19 happened. The Supreme Court ruled in the Summer following Biden taking the presidency from Trump that HERA permits FHFA and Treasury to effectively rape and pillage Fannie and Freddie at their discretion. As such, basically the only defense against this legal interpretation of HERA is to have so much capital that the companies can never be placed into conservatorship again. That's what the ERCF is and it is backed by a doubling of guarantee fees. Word on the street is that commons might not get destroyed in this equity restructuring but I'm presently not betting on it. Good luck to those that do.

I've been in this trade since 2014. I thought the courts would stand up for the law. When they didn't, I had to quit my job to raid my 401k to buy more and get multiple new jobs to work harder than ever before to make more money than ever before to buy more than ever before and prioritize payment schedules accordingly. The rest is history, I should have probably started a hedge fund (except that is impossible without a track record --- people cannot see that something will go up 20x in the coming years --- they can only see what happened this past year).

Welcome To #FANNIEGATE Part Ocho.

ACKNOWLEDGMENTS

Thank you to everyone who has made it with me this far,

I have lost many along the way who I started with,

This book is more symbolic than an actual book,

I published it because the timing was right,

Take whatever you want from it,

I believe this will be the last,

Enjoy the ride,

Love,

-Glen

TABLE OF CONTENTS

Government Incentives Align To End GSE Conservatorships	12
GSE Preferred Shares Are The Best Play On Admin Reform	16
Fannie And Freddie's Conservatorship Exit Depends On Treasury's Call	24
DC Jury Decides GSE Shareholder Contracts Breached	41
White House And Treasury Can Solve Affordability Crisis With GSEs	54
White House And Treasury Housing Leadership Should End GSE Conservatorships	60
Law, Policy, And My Journey: Fannie And Freddie's Conservatorship Unveiled	65
Inflation, Housing Crisis, And GSE Conservatorship: A Path Forward	81
Future Of Fannie Mae And Freddie Mac Post-2024 Election	94

GSE Shareholder Claims To Go To Trial This Month

Summary

- Shareholders have survived the government's motion for summary judgment, as Judge Lamberth has paved the way for shareholders to get paid for harm under the net worth sweep.
- This claim is going to trial. The trial is scheduled to begin this month and last two weeks.
- This trial and the Rop v. FHFA claims are two of the Fanniegate crowd favorites for winning litigation against the government for the net worth sweep.

Comstock/Stockbyte via Getty Images

Fannie Mae (OTCQB:FNMA) and Freddie Mac (OTCQB:FMCC) are two companies that the government took over in 2008 by placing them into conservatorship and then took all of their future money for no additional consideration in 2012. In 2019, the companies were allowed to keep their money, but the government still continues to lay claim to that money they keep. Legally speaking, the Supreme Court ruled that the law allows the government to do all of this and this basically zeroes out shareholder interests in two of the most profitable companies in America and there are a handful of pending lawsuits still fighting for shareholder rights. The purpose of this article is to highlight some shareholder friendly perspectives in Lamberth's most recent opinion.

Investment Thesis

According to the recently released legal opinion, a trial is set for October of this year. Moving forward to trial is the:

dispute of material fact as to whether the Third Amendment and its elimination of possible future dividends harmed plaintiffs by depriving them of much of the value of their shares.

The idea being that at the time of the net worth sweep, shareholder plaintiffs could not have reasonably expected the government to extinguish any possibility of them receiving any dividends ever in the future for no additional consideration, which is what the net worth sweep did. These claims are moving forward to trial. The basic idea is that shareholders are going to have to prove that their shares were going to have value absent the net worth sweep and that the government took that value because it saw that it was coming. I recommend owning preferred shares. I think these legal claims are worth $20-60B. Preferred shares have $34B of liquidation preference and if the common are worth a penny preferred are worth par. Preferred currently trade at 7-15 cents on the dollar and have significant upside on these legal claims alone.

The Lamberth Opinion

Judge Lamberth ruled that the Third Amendment eliminated any future possibility of dividends for shareholders:

The Third Amendment thus eliminated the circular-draw problem, but it also eliminated any future possibility for any non-Treasury stockholder, including plaintiffs, to receive dividends from the GSEs, because the GSEs owed their net worth to Treasury and would not take on further debt to pay dividends to other shareholders.

Judge Lamberth rules that these damage claims are going to go forward to trial in ruling against the government's motion for summary judgment:

There is no reason to preclude plaintiffs from relying on the lost-value theory in the alternative to defeat total summary judgment. The Court therefore concludes that defendants are not entitled to summary judgment in full on the question of damages, there being a lingering dispute of material fact as to whether the Third Amendment and its elimination of possible future dividends harmed plaintiffs by depriving them of much of the value of their shares. Since defendants do not specifically dispute that plaintiffs can prove the amount of damages resulting from that alleged harm, the Court has no occasion to consider that separate question at this time.

These claims are moving forward to trial. Plaintiffs' interests were effectively zeroed out by the net worth sweep whereas before the net worth sweep was implemented the junior preferred reasonably could have expected dividends to resume upon the companies eventually being able to exit conservatorship.

In Interpreting The Supreme Court Ruling

Previously Judge Lamberth ruled:

The Court finds nothing in the Plaintiffs' stock certificates suggesting they could have reasonably expected the Net Worth Sweep.

Judge Lamberth did not change his mind here based on the Supreme Court ruling and points out that the government's arguments misunderstand the context of reasonableness:

In other words, Collins does not resolve the issue here, because although reasonableness factors into both analyses, it is reasonableness with respect to different matters. At issue in Collins was whether FHFA could reasonably have determined that adopting the Third Amendment was "in the best interests of the regulated entity or the Agency," and thus acted within its statutory authority as conservator of the GSEs in so doing. Here, in contrast, the issue is whether FHFA "violated the reasonable expectations of the parties" by adopting the Third Amendment.

Lamberth is arguing that FHFA in the spirit of doing whatever it wants can enact the net worth sweep, but not without consequence. In this lawsuit that is going to trial this month, Lamberth is arguing that the net worth sweep violated the reasonable expectations of the parties. These claims are what are moving forward for a jury to decide on the facts.

Summary and Conclusion

Shareholders have won in so far as having a path towards proving harm that is heading to trial. Evidence produced by discovery supports the narrative that the reasoning behind the net worth sweep was really about seizing the profits and preventing the companies from exiting conservatorship instead of saving the then profitable companies from a death spiral.

Left to do, GSE shareholder plaintiffs will have to convince a jury that the government knew Fannie and Freddie were going to be able to retain enough earnings such that their shares would have had value under the pre-NWS capital structure. I think that the history speaks for itself. Should shareholders win, they could win par plus damages, which is why my estimates for the value of this trial is $20-60B whereas par value is $34B. This may leave some residual value for common shareholders, but I expect the bulk of the win here would accrue to junior preferred shareholders.

Government Incentives Align To End GSE Conservatorships

Summary
- Shareholders have recently lost or not prevailed in recent legal initiatives.
- The republicans have taken the house of representatives, which makes administrative action more attractive than legislation for housing finance reform.
- An analysis of Treasury's equity position shows that the government has every reason to enact administrative reform and none not to.

Alex Wong/Getty Images News

Fannie Mae (OTCQB:FNMA) and Freddie Mac (OTCQB:FMCC) are two companies in conservatorship despite having net worth in excess of what they had pre-conservatorship. Both companies were put into conservatorship in 2008, but in 2007, Freddie Mac had $27B of net worth and Fannie Mae had $45B of net worth. Now Freddie Mac has $35B and Fannie Mae has $58B of net worth because they have been able to retain earnings since September 2019. The definition of conservatorship from FHFA's own website:

Fannie Mae and Freddie Mac are in conservatorship to preserve and conserve their assets and property and restore them to a sound and solvent condition so they can continue to fulfill their statutory missions.

Treasury's equity interests in Fannie and Freddie are currently preventing FHFA from restoring Fannie and Freddie by preventing them from being able to raise enough capital to become adequately capitalized and exit conservatorship.

Investment Thesis

Fannie and Freddie have more money now than they did before they were placed into conservatorship and are on track to continue to accumulate money on their path to having more than they ever had in history. They are now in a position where, if they could raise money via equity offerings, they could exit conservatorship. Treasury's equity interest, which lays claim to every cent of earnings that accrues to Fannie and Freddie, actively impedes this. Despite having more money than before, the government so far has refused to let go of Fannie Mae and Freddie Mac. On an economic basis, the government is not getting paid anything for its equity investment and only the political party in charge of the White House has any say in how Fannie and Freddie are run. When the Trump admin ended, Biden took over and took complete control and put in his changes. Eventually, a different president with different political objectives for Fannie and Freddie will take office. The idea is that only the president that actually ends the conservatorships gets to lock in their vision of reform and gets to spend the money trapped in Treasury's equity positions of Fannie and Freddie. The Trump administration did the heavy lifting of starting the retention of capital and Trump said:

My administration would have also sold the government's common stock in these companies at a huge profit

Now, Biden is in power, but he won't be forever. An investment in Fannie and Freddie junior preferred stock is a bet on an eventual restructuring of the equity where a president wants to fund an initiative and accomplish housing finance reform. With interest rates rising significantly this past year and republicans taking the house, the next 12 months are ripe for administrative action.

Junior preferred stock trades at less than 10 cents on the dollar but would be made whole if the government restructures its equity so that it can lock reform and spend its profits.

Capital Planning Rule

Under Biden's Sandra Thompson, FHFA proposed a capital rule 12/27/2021 where FHFA asserted that it may require Fannie and Freddie to develop and implement capital restoration plans:

For example, pursuant to FHFA's Prompt Corrective Action and general enforcement authority, it may require an Enterprise to develop and implement a capital restoration plan, restrict asset growth or activities, and take other appropriate actions to remediate the violation of law.

FHFA argued that despite the SPSPA preventing Fannie and Freddie from holding anywhere near the capital FHFA's ECRF requires, this new rule would allow the Enterprises to close the gap by sorting out a capital raising framework:

The Enterprises are currently in conservatorship, are subject to the restrictions of the Senior Preferred Stock Purchase Agreements between them and the U.S. Treasury, and do not hold capital anywhere near the levels specified in the ERCF. The capital plans will allow the Enterprises to identify the amount of capital they need to raise to close the gap with the ERCF, and to consider the timing of when to raise capital, and what types of capital to raise.

FHFA went on to finalize this capital planning rule June 2022. The first plan submissions under this new rule are due May 20, 2023. Execution of the GSE capital plans gets them out of conservatorship.

Recent Shareholder Based Litigation

Shareholders have fought FHFA's actions during conservatorship that have largely zeroed out the economic interest of non-governmental shareholders have sued the government and the companies primarily for the net worth sweep.

Collins v. Yellen

Judge Ellison ruled that Trump's memo doesn't matter and dismissed the constitutional claims that were remanded back down from the Supreme Court which seemed to argue that if Trump did put out such a statement that shareholder plaintiffs could use it to show harm. Judge Ellison dismissed all plaintiff claims even though they had been remanded back down from the Supreme Court. I expect that this ruling gets appealed back to en banc.

Rop v. FHFA

The sixth circuit court of appeals ruled that Ed DeMarco was not serving in violation of the Appointment's Clause when he enacted the net worth sweep. This was a win for the government and a loss for shareholders. I expect this will get petitioned to the Supreme Court.

Lamberth Trial

Shareholders had breach of contract claims go to trial in October. The result was a hung jury. I expect this will go for a re-trial. My understanding is that plaintiffs will get to re-submit their reliance damage model. I think the jury was confused by the share loss damage model. Ed DeMarco and the government bragged that they didn't really do any research or get any second opinions when enacting the net worth sweep, which they said was to save the mortgage market, but the jury seemed unable to determine if that was arbitrary or met any standard of due diligence.

Summary and Conclusion

The republicans just took the house of representatives. The only housing finance reform option from here on out is administrative. The government is incentivized by $100B to enact it and as a bonus gets to lock in its view on reform. If the Biden administration does not take action, they'll lose the opportunity to lock in their view of reform and the next administration could change housing finance completely and spend the $100B on completely different objectives. As such, the government is strongly incentivized to take action since inaction hands the ball possibly to the opposing team. The junior preferreds trade at less than 10 cents on the dollar which seems to be pricing in an understanding that not only has Biden's Treasury not yet restructured its equity in Fannie and Freddie, but that it won't and every administration in the future will not as well. On top of this, it assigns a low probability for winning any of shareholder litigation.

I think the Biden administration aligns with all its incentives and takes action on housing finance reform.

GSE Preferred Shares Are The Best Play On Admin Reform

Summary

- On January 9, 2023, the Supreme Court denied writ of certiorari on the Takings Claim.
- The potential massive dilution of common shares may seem negative for current common shareholders, but it ultimately maximizes the size of the government's ownership stake.
- Junior preferred stock interests cannot be diluted, and with the companies retaining earnings, the only real path forward makes them whole, the only question is when.

ablokhin

Fannie Mae (OTCQB:FNMA) and Freddie Mac (OTCQB:FMCC), two government-sponsored enterprises (GSEs), play a crucial role in the US housing market. They have a long history of providing liquidity and stability to the mortgage market by purchasing mortgages from banks and other lenders, and then packaging them into securities that are sold to investors. However, their future has been uncertain since they were taken under government conservatorship during the 2008 financial crisis. This article will examine the current state of Fannie Mae and Freddie Mac, their role in the housing market, and the potential implications of privatizing them.

Investment Thesis

It is important to note that there is no pending legal action that would require a liquidation preference writedown, such as the Takings lawsuit, which was not taken up by the Supreme Court. In other words, no lawsuit challenges the net worth sweep. Moving forward, the only restructuring path forward from the government's perspective is thus to convert its stake as there is no pending litigation that gets resolved by writing it down and thus no legal reason for the government to do so. As such, common shares are a gamble on whether the government thinks capital markets will be more receptive of GSE equity offerings if it gives a little. This is a gamble I'm not willing to make.

The conversion of the liquidation preference of the Senior Preferred Stock Purchase Agreements (SPSPAs), along with the exercise of warrants and the raising of capital, has the potential to dilute common shares by over 99%. This outcome maximizes the government's ownership stake and thus looks to ultimately be in the best interest of the government. The preferred stock, currently trading at 5-10% of their par value, have the potential to trade up to 100% of their par value in an equity restructuring that allows them to raise capital. This highlights the potential for significant gains for investors in the preferred stock, particularly in light of the current state of the Fannie Mae and Freddie Mac being that they have been prepared to exit conservatorship by FHFA but are priced as if it's never going to happen.

The Case For Admin Reform

Reprivatizing Fannie Mae and Freddie Mac is beneficial for both housing and the government. Firstly, as the government-sponsored enterprises (GSEs), they play a crucial role in the U.S. housing market by providing financing to lenders for nearly half of current U.S. mortgages. This is done by buying mortgages from lenders and packaging and selling them to investors, which makes mortgages cheaper and more available across the country.

Secondly, conservatorship has created an opportunity for addressing the nation's affordable housing crisis and advancing racial equity in housing. The government received stock interests in the GSEs valued at $48 to $98 billion by the Congressional Budget Office. These assets should be used to support the GSEs' public mission, particularly by exchanging them for a commitment by the GSEs to additional affordable housing measures and a restorative justice housing program that provides targeted down payment and other assistance aimed at closing the racial homeownership gap.

Thirdly, a utility oversight structure is the best structure for the GSEs going forward. It enables them to provide critical relief to the housing market and the overall economy during a crisis, and to advance their public mission in regular times. This structure should be implemented permanently to secure the GSEs as an emergency backstop, and to enhance their operation and oversight.

It is important to note that many of the proposed changes to Fannie Mae and Freddie Mac can be implemented through administrative reform, rather than requiring action from Congress. This includes increasing affordable housing support, implementing racial equity programs, and solidifying utility oversight. The main area where congressional action would be necessary is if the decision was made to implement a security level guarantee, which would provide an explicit government guarantee on the GSEs' securities. This would be a significant shift from the current implicit guarantee / corporate level guarantee and would require legislation to authorize and implement. However, by utilizing administrative reform for other reforms, progress can be made in improving the GSEs' operations and fulfilling their public mission while discussions on a security level guarantee continue.

It is worth noting that I do believe that the path to utility model includes preserving the remaining limited explicit government backstop for Fannie and Freddie at the enterprise level, and that Fannie and Freddie will likely have to pay for this moving forward instead of it being free like it was pre-2008.

Why 2023 Feels Ripe For Admin Reform

The current administration has made it clear that they are committed to addressing the affordable housing crisis and advancing racial equity in the housing market. Reprivatizing Fannie Mae and Freddie Mac, and ensuring they are better equipped to serve their public mission, could be a key part of this effort. In recent years, administrative reform of the GSEs has been ongoing and the Federal Housing Finance Agency (FHFA) has hastened the process of releasing them from conservatorship.

Additionally, the political landscape also appears favorable for administrative reform this year. The current administration has a majority in the Senate but not in the House of Representatives, which can help to facilitate the passage of any necessary administrative actions because legislative options are less available with a split House and Senate. Furthermore, there is a growing consensus among policymakers, industry experts, and advocacy groups that the GSEs need to be reformed in order to address the affordable housing crisis and advance racial equity in the housing market.

The GSEs have played a crucial role in providing relief to the housing market during the COVID crisis. Hence, it is likely that the administration will want to solidify and formalize the GSEs' role in addressing the affordable housing crisis and advancing racial equity and this can be accomplished as part of exiting conservatorship via consent decree.

In summary, the current administration's commitment to address the affordable housing crisis, the favorable political landscape, and the urgency of the current economic condition, all point towards the possibility of near term administrative reform of the GSEs.

Capital Restoration Plans Due This Year

The formalization of the capital planning rule was an important step towards the reprivatization of Fannie Mae and Freddie Mac.

Under the final rule, each Enterprise will submit its first capital plan by May 20, 2023.

The rule, which has been developed by the Federal Housing Finance Agency (FHFA), set clear guidelines and will help Fannie and Freddie access capital markets. This will enable Fannie Mae and Freddie Mac to raise the capital they need to operate and support the housing market, which is crucial for their ability to fulfill their public mission of advancing affordable housing. This will enable them to secure the GSEs as an emergency backstop during a crisis, enhance operation of the GSEs in regular times, and advance the GSEs' public mission. It will also help to ensure that the GSEs have the resources they need to continue providing financing to lenders for nearly half of current U.S. mortgages by buying the mortgages from lenders and packaging and selling them to investors, making mortgages cheaper and more available across the country. A capital restoration plan would only have significance if the GSEs equity was restructured in order to attract a capital raise so it is interesting that Sandra Thompson finalized the capital planning rule under Biden.

FHFA's 2022 Performance And Accountability Report

In November 2022, FHFA released a report outlining that FHFA had accomplished their strategic objectives associated with their responsibility to end the conservatorships of the Enterprises:

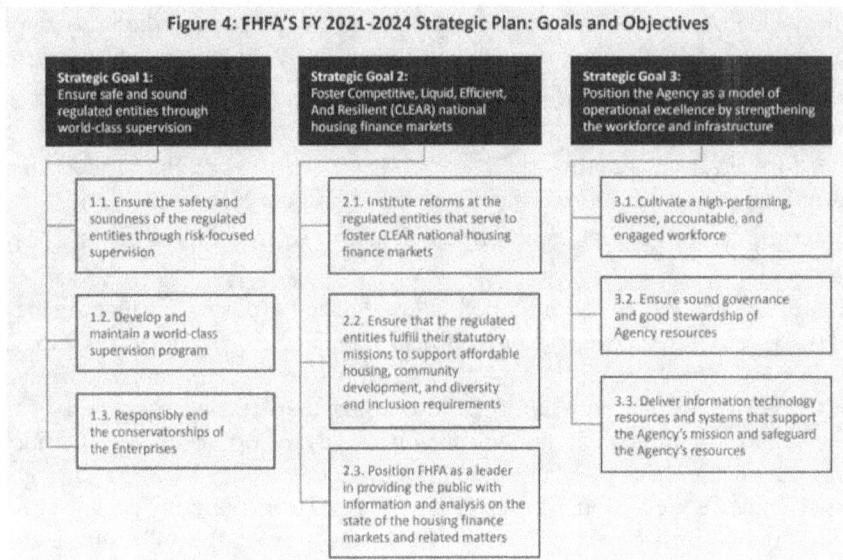

Figure 4: FHFA'S FY 2021-2024 Strategic Plan: Goals and Objectives

- **FHFA Strategic Plan: Goals and Objectives (FHFA)**

FHFA reported that it met all its strategic objectives with respect to this strategic goal in 2022:

STRATEGIC OBJECTIVE 1.3: RESPONSIBLY END THE CONSERVATORSHIPS OF THE ENTERPRISES

FHFA continues to focus on managing the ongoing conservatorships to preserve and conserve the assets of the Enterprises for the benefit of the taxpayers, as well as reducing taxpayer risk from Enterprise operations. In FY 2022, FHFA monitored two performance measures for Strategic Objective 1.3 and met the targets for both of these measures. The table below reports progress on these measures.

Table 10: Strategic Objective 1.3 – Summary of Performance Measures and Results

Strategic Objective 1.3: Responsibly end the conservatorships of the Enterprises

Performance Measure	FY 2017	FY 2018	FY 2019	FY 2020	FY 2021	FY 2022 Target	FY 2022 Result
1.3.1: Issue a proposed rule on Enterprise disclosures under the Enterprise Regulatory Capital Framework	N/A[23]	N/A	N/A	N/A	N/A	FY 2022	MET
1.3.2: Issue a proposed rule on Enterprise Capital Planning	N/A	N/A	N/A	N/A	N/A	FY 2022	MET

- **Strategic Objective 1.3 Responsibly End the conservatorships (FHFA)**

FHFA finalized all the rules that needed to be complete in order to responsibly end the conservatorships of Fannie and Freddie. The proposed rule on Enterprise Capital Planning was subsequently elevated and put into action in the sequential strategic plan.

FHFA's 2022-2026 Strategic Plan

FHFA updated their strategic plan under Sandra Thompson. Instead of creating the rule for enterprise capital planning, now FHFA has moved forward to include Strategic Objective 1.3.3:

Oversee the Enterprises' implementation of capital plans to achieve regulatory capital requirements

Sandra Thompson's director's message reads:

FHFA is continuing to take incremental steps to strengthen the capital positions of Fannie Mae and Freddie Mac (together, "the Enterprises") so that they can fulfill their responsibilities throughout the economic cycle. FHFA recently finalized important enhancements to the Enterprise Regulatory Capital Framework that provide the Enterprises with the necessary incentives to transfer credit risk to private investors, which will help protect taxpayers from the risks posed by the Enterprises and support the Enterprises in facilitating equitable and sustainable access to mortgage credit. Furthermore, FHFA proposed additional capital planning and disclosure requirements to help ensure the Enterprises have robust systems and processes in place to achieve and maintain proper levels of capital.

Implementing capital plans that achieve regulatory capital requirements ends the conservatorship by recapitalization and release. Fannie and Freddie have been retaining earnings since 2019 and with every continued step to strengthen their capital positions continues to affirm that receivership is not a viable restructuring option moving forward.

The Government's Valuing of Junior Preferreds

In the government's recapitalization report, it outlines the effects of ending the conservatorships in 2023 and 2025. In fact, the only way to wipe the junior preferred is through receivership:

If, however, the Treasury wanted to raise capital through the sale of new common shares without resorting to receivership for the GSEs, the claims of junior preferred shareholders would have to be addressed.

In the two infographics below, the government shows that the junior preferred are made whole in scenarios where the SPSPA is worth less than face value and where the government's warrants are worthless (denoted with an asterisk *).

2023

Table 2.
Scenarios for Recapitalization With a Common-Stock Offering at the Beginning of 2023

	Scenario 1	Scenario 2	Scenario 3
	Parameters of the Scenario		
Earnings Retention Period (Years)	3	3	3
Capital Requirement (As a percentage of unadjusted assets)	3	4.5	6
Investors' Required Return on Capital (Percent)	8	10	12
Annual Growth Rate of Earnings for First Five Years After Recapitalization (Percent)	8	4	0
	Results of the Scenario (Billions of dollars)		
Amount of Capital Required	185	278	370
Minus: Capital on Hand at the End of 2022	78	78	78
Equals: Capital Shortfall at the End of 2022	107	200	292
GSEs' Total Equity Value (Amount available from sale of common stock)	402	283	224
Amount Available After Covering Capital Shortfall	294	83	-69
Amount of the Treasury's senior preferred shares redeemed (Total face value of $190 billion)	190	48	0
Amount of investors' junior preferred shares redeemed (Total face value of $35 billion)	35	35	0
Value of the Treasury's warrants^a	55	*	0

- **2023 Recapitalization Plan (CBO GOV)**

2025

Table 3.
Scenarios for Recapitalization With a Common-Stock Offering at the Beginning of 2025

	Scenario 1	Scenario 2	Scenario 3
	Parameters of the Scenario		
Earnings Retention Period (Years)	5	5	5
Capital Requirement (As a percentage of unadjusted assets)	3	4.5	6
Investors' Required Return on Capital (Percent)	8	10	12
Annual Growth Rate of Earnings for First Five Years After Recapitalization (Percent)	8	4	0
	Results of the Scenario (Billions of dollars)		
Amount of Capital Required	200	300	400
Minus: Capital on Hand at the End of 2024	128	128	128
Equals: Capital Shortfall at the End of 2024	72	172	273
GSEs' Total Equity Value (Amount available from sale of common stock)	434	306	242
Amount Available After Covering Capital Shortfall	362	133	-31
Amount of the Treasury's senior preferred shares redeemed (Total face value of $190 billion)	190	98	0
Amount of investors' junior preferred shares redeemed (Total face value of $35 billion)	35	35	0
Value of the Treasury's warrants^a	110	*	0

- **2025 Recapitalization Plan (CBO GOV)**

Junior preferred take priority to the government's stake in a recapitalization according to the government reports. The CBO report continues to outline converting its preferred to common as a restructuring option:

One way in which the Treasury could modify the agreements would be to convert its preferred shares into common shares, into warrants for common shares, or into some form of debt in the GSEs

With the Supreme Court's recent ruling, there is no pending litigation that would prevent SPSPA conversion. Further, the government outlines that it has taken this path before in footnote 24:

Converting preferred shares into common shares would be similar to the approach that the Treasury took during the financial crisis when it intervened to help other firms, such as the American International Group, known as AIG.

As such, I expect this to result in substantial dilution to existing common, making them uninvestable as there is no security in the face of the pending restructuring that is a necessary step to raising new third party capital.

Summary and Conclusion

In conclusion, Fannie Mae and Freddie Mac's preferred stock presents a potential opportunity for investors, due to the potential for significant value appreciation through an equity restructuring that allows them to raise capital. This restructuring, which may involve the conversion of the liquidation preference of the SPSPAs and the exercise of warrants held by the Treasury, would dilute the value of existing common shares but would be done to maximize the size and value of the government's ownership stake. As such, this outcome is likely to be in the best interest of the government and ultimately, the stability of the U.S housing market. In this fashion of security analysis and buying those that have security and value that can be deduced, common have no security and are akin to a gamble on the government's perspective, informed by investment bankers, as to whether or not converting the SPSPA or the mechanics therein, maximizes the value of its equity stake. The preferred on the other hand are money good in a recapitalization by the governments own admission in its own documents. Plan accordingly.

Fannie And Freddie's Conservatorship Exit Depends On Treasury's Call

Apr. 13, 2023 12:09 AM ET Federal Home Loan Mortgage Corporation PFD 8.375% NCM (FMCKJ) Stock, FNMAS Stock FMCC, FMCCG, FMCCH, FMCCI, FMCCK, FMCCL, FMCCM, FMCCN, FMCCO, FMCCP, FMCCS, FMCCT, FMCKI, FMCKK, FMCKL, FMCKM, FMCKN, FMCKO, FMCKP, FNMA, FNMAG, FNMAH, FNMAJ, FNMAK, FNMAM, FNMAN, FNMAP, FNMAT, FNMFM, FNMFN, FNMFO, FREJP

Summary

- Mark Calabria published the book Shelter From The Storm, which has some insights that investors can use to shelter from the storm of a restructuring of the GSE balance sheets.
- Calabria believes the single most important action he could have taken during his tenure as FHFA director was to end the profit sweep, which he formalized in September 2019.
- Calabria talks about how FHFA and the GSEs were ready to conduct a restructuring by late summer 2020 but was put on hold until after the elections.
- According to government valuation reports, Fannie and Freddie junior preferreds get made whole in any restructuring outside receivership that results in an equity offering.

Win McNamee/Getty Images News

Fannie Mae (OTCQB:FNMA) and Freddie Mac (OTCQB:FMCC) are two companies that have been in conservatorship since 2008. The conservatorship is run by the Federal Housing Finance Agency (FHFA) who is currently directed by Sandra Thompson who was preceded by Mark Calabria. Mark Calabria helped draft HERA which converted the OFHEO into the FHFA. So, it is correct to say that he wrote the law that brought into existence the agency that he was put in charge of during the Trump administration. Further, before being put in as head of FHFA, he wrote a white paper on his view that the net worth sweep was illegal. The Supreme Court proceeded to not only disagree with him, not only ruling that the net worth sweep was legal but also that he could be fired as FHFA is not an independent agency but serves at the direction of the president, making FHFA director a political appointee position.

Mark Calabria recently published a book entitled Shelter From The Storm that is a hero's story that walks the reader through all of his learning experiences along the way and gives various insights into his approach and musings. This book offers investors a peak behind the curtain.

Investment Thesis

By process of elimination the conservatorships have three paths forward:
1. Never ending conservatorships
2. Conservatorships that end in receivership
3. Conservatorships that end with the companies adequately capitalized and a return of private capital that protects taxpayers

The actions taken by Mnuchin and Calabria eliminated option 1 and effectively eliminated option 2 from the agenda and charted the course for option 3. I say effectively eliminated option 2 because the only way receivership is a realistic possibility at this point is Yellowstone erupts or an asteroid hits the United States and wipes out a 200+ mile radius in my view. In Calabria's view the greatest threat would be significant sea level rise through Global Warming. Absent life altering climate events, this leaves option 3 as the only realistic outcome and the only question is when. People seem to think that "not this decade" is the right answer here based on the current pricing of Fannie and Freddie equity securities. Mark Calabria is not as optimistic about Biden administrative housing reform as I am, and I think that the only investible securities to capitalize on administrative reform are Fannie and Freddie preferred securities like S series of Fannie (OTCQB:FNMAS) or Z series of Freddie (OTCQB:FMCKJ) which I think would see face value of $25 in a restructuring via conversion to common at the IPO price. I commonly refer to the junior preferred stock like FNMAS as JPS.

History and Risks To Junior Preferred

Junior preferred shares were all issued at face value before the imposition of conservatorship in 2008. The imposition of conservatorship collapsed prices to 31 cents in 2010. Prices gradually recovered to $10 in 2014 when the first Lamberth ruling was anticipated to rule in favor of plaintiffs' interpretation of the law but failed to do so and prices collapsed again below $5 for a few years:

FNMAS Stock Price Chart (Google)

Trump became president in 2017 and was believed to favor admin driven recap and release and in September of 2019 Plaintiffs won a legal ruling that the net worth sweep was illegal. In 2021, Trump's Mnuchin and Calabria couldn't finish the restructuring and the Supreme Court overturned the earlier ruling saying that the net worth sweep is legal. Earlier this year, the Supreme Court also decided to not take up the Takings case for review. In conclusion, the Supreme Court seems to support the notion that the government taking the net worth of a private company in conservatorship is both legal and not a takings.

Last 12 Months

In the last 12 months and more recently, no one can exit fast enough. The selling has been relentless:

FNMAS 12 month stock price chart (Google)

Bear Cases

The companies could be placed into receivership to get around the JPS. The conservatorship could last forever to get around having to deal with the JPS. In my view, GSE equities would also have no economic value if the SPSPA is never restructured (from Fannie's 10-K):

> **Dividend Amount Following Capital Reserve End Date**
>
> Beginning on the first dividend period following the capital reserve end date, the applicable quarterly dividend amount on the senior preferred stock will be the lesser of:
>
> (1) a 10% annual rate on the then-current liquidation preference of the senior preferred stock; and
>
> (2) an amount equal to the incremental increase in our net worth during the immediately prior fiscal quarter.
>
> However, the applicable quarterly dividend amount will immediately increase to a 12% annual rate on the then-current liquidation preference of the senior preferred stock if we fail to timely pay dividends in cash to Treasury. This increased dividend amount will continue until the dividend period following the date we have paid, in cash, full cumulative dividends to Treasury (including any unpaid dividends), at which point the applicable quarterly dividend amount will revert to the prior calculation method.

10 K Fannie Mae NWS Takes Everything (Fannie Mae 10-K)

Long story short, if the government does not restructure its equity, common and junior preferred are likely worthless. I think that this combined with all the lost litigation paints a pretty bleak picture which is why the junior preferred have collapsed to 52-week lows.

Lastly, in a restructuring of the government's equity that is outside of receivership where the Junior Preferred shareholders are willing to accept less than face value, as it is better to take a little something than a whole lot of nothing, the end result for junior preferred may be subpar. I don't think this perspective carries water but it is a perspective nonetheless.

Agreement To Restructure Treasury's Investment

In early 2021 Treasury signed an agreement with both Fannie and Freddie where they committed:

to work to restructure Treasury's investment and dividend amount in a matter that facilitates the orderly exit from conservatorship, ensures Treasury is appropriately compensated, and permits the Enterprise to raise third-party capital and make distributions as appropriate.

In my view the light at the end of the tunnel is that FHFA under Sandra Thompson continued down this path and finalized a capital planning rule.

Capital Planning Rule Sets Stage For Capital Raise

Requiring financial institutions to file capital plans implies the intention to allow them to raise capital. In my opinion, the SPSPA in its current unrestructured state renders the capital planning rule ineffective because it prohibits companies from raising capital, which defeats the purpose of having such a rule. However, this situation is still a work in progress as evidenced by their continued work based on FHFA's performance assessment in Fannie's 10-K:

FHFA raised a concern in connection with our implementation of our capital plan, noting that we continue to work through the errors in a model we use to forecast.

Capital plans have been formalized under Sandra Thompson as preparation for life after conservatorship. This would theoretically pick up where Calabria and Mnuchin left off with the SPSPA work.

Calabria To Sandra Thompson

Calabria points out in his book the progress of the restructuring plans that he had worked on that are still workable on the shelf:

Since we had well-developed restructuring plans by late summer 2020, why did none of them happen? First, I believe both the Treasury and the White House wanted to push the issue until after the election.

...

Whether the continued back-and-forth with Treasury was in good faith on their part, I will never know. What I do know is that there was a general agreement between the FHFA and Treasury on a restructuring plan. That would not immediately end the conservatorship, but it would place the companies in a position to raise outside equity, which I could complete later in 2021, depending on market conditions.

Calabria's successor Sandra Thompson has since finalized the Capital Planning Rule June 1, 2022 which requires the GSEs to submit capital plans May 20, 2023.

The final rule's requirement to develop capital plans will allow the Enterprises to identify the amount of capital they need to raise to meet the ERCF's requirements, and to consider the timing of when to raise capital

In November 2022, FHFA reported that it issued this rule and successfully met this target as part of responsibly ending the conservatorships as well as completing the proposed rule on Enterprise disclosures under the ERCF. Now, FHFA is to "(o)versee the Enterprises' implementation of capital plans to achieve regulatory capital requirements." It is impossible for FHFA to achieve this objective of the companies achieving regulatory capital requirements before the end of FHFA's Strategic Plan 2022-2026 window without leveraging their capital plans to raise third party capital.

Sandra Thompson appears to have carried on with Calabria's plans of following the law and preparing Fannie and Freddie to raise capital and exit conservatorship.

The CBO Report Acknowledges Value In A Restructuring

The CBO report talks to the junior preferred stock still having value in a restructuring that doesn't involve receivership, implying that the only way junior preferred do not see face value is through receivership:

If, however, the Treasury wanted to raise capital through the sale of new common shares without resorting to receivership for the GSEs, the claims of junior preferred shareholders would have to be addressed. In this analysis, those shareholders are paid the full $35 billion face value of their shares from the proceeds of the common-stock sale, if possible, thus retiring their claims on the assets and income of the recapitalized GSEs.

Why would JPS get paid face value? The CBO addresses this too:

Junior preferred shareholders are in line to receive the dividends associated with their shares before holders of new or existing common shares. Thus, they might refuse to allow the GSEs to retire their claims on the GSEs' assets and income at less than the face value of their shares in the lead-up to a sale of new common stock. That refusal would reduce the value of the new common shares, making recapitalization more difficult. Even though the Treasury's preferred shares have seniority over the preconservatorship preferred shares owned by investors, the Treasury would have an incentive to make an arrangement that took into account its ownership stake in the GSEs' common stock.

Mark Calabria talks about the scenario where all preferred convert to common:

A conversion of all preferred equity was one of the only ways to fix the companies' balance sheets in a manner acceptable to Treasury.

In this scenario, junior preferred would only agree to convert to common if they get par in my opinion. Otherwise, there is no reason to convert at all when dividends will resume on the government's post-restructured common stock. Obviously, market prices point to other investors having significantly different opinions than mine.

Is The Only Question: When?

Mark Calabria celebrated this outcome in his book:

Therefore, one of my first responsibilities as director was to end the profit sweep, a action that was formalized in a September 2019 agreement with Treasury. There was essentially no profit sweep during my tenure. We were building capital at the companies, as was so clearly intended by Congress. I believe that was the single most important action I could have taken to address the illegality of the third amendment.

Building capital at the companies, with an eye toward eventual release from conservatorship, had occasionally been presented as some personal agenda of mine. It was not. It was clearly what the statute required and Congress intended.

By ending the profit sweep, Calabria and Mnuchin ended the stealth receivership and turned the conservatorship back into a conservatorship. Since junior preferred get face value in any exit from conservatorship that does not pass through the chop shop of receivership and the companies have retained earnings since 2019 and now have more capital than at any point in their history; the only real question to ask is when the companies are going to finally exit conservatorship. Calabria suggested in his book that the reason Mnuchin and he were not able to finish the equity restructuring was because Mnuchin did not want to upset Janet Yellen:

Any restructuring, to be successful, would have offended somebody. We did not get it done because Mnuchin did not want to upset anyone on his way out the door, including incoming Treasury secretary Janet Yellen.

When Mark Calabria and Mnuchin met with Biden's Janet Yellen to go over continuing Calabria's vision of ending the conservatorships, Calabria writes that he does not expect Yellen to move on administrative housing reform:

I repeatedly raised my concerns about the mortgage and housing markets, both to Treasury directly and to the Financial Stability Oversight Council. I also emphasized that no part of our financial system was more vulnerable to climate change than the mortgage market. If we were to see significant coastal erosion, the losses to Fannie and Freddie could be extraordinary. Unfortunately, the response was generally a dull, polite smile and nod. It appeared that new Treasury leadership would ignore the growing risks in our mortgage finance system.

Needless to say, Calabria does not think the Biden administration is interested in using its equity position in Fannie and Freddie to achieve its policy goals during a split Congress.

Pending Litigation Calendar

There is still ongoing litigation challenging government actions surrounding the net worth sweep. The most recent shareholder produced calendar is below:

GSEs - Litigation Calendar

	2023			
	Apr	May	Jun	Q3	Q4
[1] Trial (7/24/23 - 8/4/23) Trial Verdict Expected (~8/7/23)					
[2] Defendants Reply Brief (4/3/23) Plaintiffs Final Brief (~4/24/23) Oral Arguments (~Q2 23) Decision Expected (~Q3 '23)					
[3] Defendants Reply Brief (4/7/23) Plaintiffs Final Brief (~4/28/23) SCOTUS Petition Decision (~Q2 '23)					
[4] Defendants Reply Brief (5/3/23) Plaintiffs Final Brief (~5/24/23) Oral Arguments (~Q3 23) Decision Expected (~Q4 '23)					
[5] Defendants Response (4/21/23) Decision Expected (~Q4 23)					
Quinn Amended Complaint (4/14/23) Decision Expected (~Q4 '23)					
Wazee En Banc Petition(s) (~Q3 '23)					
Fisher En Banc Petition (~Q3 '23)					

[1] *Consolidated v. FHFA/GSEs (Claim: Contracts implied covenant)*
[2] *Collins v. Yellen (Claim: Removal provision remedy + Appropriations clause)*
[3] *Rop v. FHFA (Claim: Appointments clause)*
[4] *Bhatti v. FHFA (Claim: Removal provision remedy)*
[5] *COFC: Kelly v. US (Claim: Takings, JPS Contracts)*
COFC: Quinn (Claim: Takings)
COFC: Wazee (Claim: Takings, Unjust Enrichment)
COFC: Bryndon Fisher (Claim: Takings)

GSE Shareholder Litigation Calendar (Familymang)

From above, I think the COFC lawsuits are now a long shot since the Supreme Court did not take them up and the appeals court outright dismissed them. The contract claims litigation pending in Lamberth's court is worth a few bucks for the preferred at best, I think, although I think that there is room pending a victory there to appeal Lamberth's rulings that pigeonholed the plaintiffs' claims to only being a few bucks instead of face value. The Collins case is probably the most interesting because we know that the en banc appeals court there ruled favorably for the plaintiffs on the APA claims before the SCOTUS reversed that ruling.

CapWealth's Tim Pagliara On Admin Reform

In December, GSE preferred investor Tim Pagliara said he believes the timing for possible admin reform start taking shape in the first 6 months of 2023.

At the end of Q1 he put out an update that continued to support the concept that 2023 could be the year for Fannie and Freddie preferred shareholders.

Tim Pagliara has been an activist shareholder fighting for Fannie and Freddie to be released from conservatorship.

Bill Ackman's Pershing Square Holdings On Admin Reform

In his 2022 annual report Bill Ackman agrees that it is not if, but when the companies will exit from conservatorship:

Fannie Mae and Freddie Mac remain valuable perpetual options on the companies' exit from conservatorship.

...

We believe that it is simply a matter of when, not if, that Fannie and Freddie will be released from conservatorship.

Bill Ackman is really the reason behind why I started buying Fannie and Freddie equities to begin with back in 2014 and I agree with his perspective that it is just a matter of when.

Sayers Research Report

Kyle Nisbet thinks that Fannie and Freddie will likely be released from conservatorship in the next two years:

Despite currently being in conservatorship, whether by executive action or the result of a legal case, I believe it's likely that Fannie Mae & Freddie Mac will be released from conservatorship in the next 2 years, and should that happen the preferred shares would receive par value (from 6.88% of par currently) and there exist various opportunities for very high upside with the common shares.

Kyle's upside analysis on the common shares basically requires a legal victory or that Treasury voluntarily gives up the value of its SPSPA, something that Calabria notes that Treasury says is illegal.

Prior Fannie Mae CFO Timothy J Howard

In the comments section of Tim's "A Political Problem" blog post on Fannie and Freddie suggests that Calhoun being chosen by the White House originally to lead FHFA is compelling evidence that someone in the administration saw recap and release as good public policy:

But…the fact that Calhoun was nominated at all is compelling evidence that some person, or group of people, in the administration 18 months ago was (or were) aware that having him lead Fannie and Freddie out of conservatorship, and restore them as "real companies" providing low-cost affordable housing financing was good public policy for the President's party.

Tim Howard suggests that whomever was behind this push for Calhoun may be able to prevail in achieving administrative housing reform under Biden.

I suspect that whomever was behind the nomination of Calhoun in the first year of the Biden administration will see if they can't knit together a coalition of policy officials confident enough in the benefits of recapitalizing (under a true risk-based standard) and releasing Fannie and Freddie as healthy, management-run companies to be able to take on the fight with FE leaders they know is coming once they make their proposed policy public. But we'll only hear from them if and when they think they've reached a "tipping point," and believe they have a decent shot at prevailing.

Tim Howard puts the probability of a Biden solution at 50-50:

Am I predicting this will happen? If I'm being honest with myself, I'd have to say —to use a legal phrase—that I still think it's "more likely than not" the status quo will persist during the remaining term of this administration. But I also think the chances of a favorable resolution to the conservatorships in the next 20 months are well above zero, and may be closer to 50-50.

Meanwhile, the market is pricing odds closer to 5-10% of administrative reform under Biden.

Independent Community Bankers of America

The ICBA is requesting the FHFA and Treasury expand efforts to resolve the government's ownership stake:

ICBA and the nation's community banks strongly urge the Federal Housing Finance Agency and the U.S. Treasury to expand efforts to resolve the government's ownership of Fannie Mae and Freddie Mac and set them on a path to raise capital and eventually exit conservatorship.

...

We therefore urge FHFA Director Sandra Thompson and Treasury Secretary Janet Yellen to take immediate action to resolve Treasury's ownership based on the Preferred Stock Purchase Agreements with the goal of allowing the GSEs to access the capital markets and to eventually exit conservatorship.

Mark Calabria wrote a tweet March 21 arguing that the ICBA is stronger than the TBTF banks:

Mark Calabria @MarkCalabria · Mar 21
Replying to @jasonfurman
100% my experience as staff on Senate Banking Committee- ICBA rolls big banks everyday - as I discussed a decade ago...

congressmen than a large out-of-state bank. Anyone ᴡ
thinks that say JP Morgan has a lot of pull has never ɢ
up against the Independent Community Bankers of Ar
(ICBA). Believe me, from having been in those fights, I
makes JP Morgan look politically weak (just read all tʜ
small bank exemptions in Dodd-Frank).

Perhaps the most compelling evidence to me is that n
of the really bad features of our financial regulatory sʏ
were the result of lobbying efforts by small banks. Suᴄ
disasters as Fannie Mae, Freddie Mac, the Federal Ho
Loan Banks, the FDIC, or restrictions on branch-bankɪ
(thankfully now gone) all came about from the deman
small banks. The large banks (and FDR) for instance

Mark Calabria tweets about ICBA (Twitter)

Senate democrats are even writing the administration requesting a "whole-of-government" approach to address our nation's housing needs. Monetizing the government's equity position could help achieve that goal.

Sandra Thompson On What's Next for FHFA

From minute 27-32 of the Bipartisan Policy Center's Fireside Chat with Acting Director Sandra L. Thompson, Sandra Thompson spoke to housing finance reform. The first thing Sandra Thompson addresses is that no one expected the enterprises to be in conservatorship for 14+ years. She points to the regime change under Calabria where the companies retain capital. Her big ticket items list starts with conversations with Treasury as a significant shareholder have to take place and there have been precedential conversations.

One of the things that we are doing is we are preparing the Enterprises to adjust to supervision in a way that they would be regulated outside of conservatorship.

...

If they ever get out of conservatorship everybody knows that it's going to be the largest IPO ever.

Sandra Thompson's preparation of the GSEs for life after conservatorship in conjunction with her finalization of the capital planning rule makes it sound like her conversations with Treasury probably did not revolve around a never ending conservatorship.

On Timing

We are in the second half of the Biden administration. FHFA delayed the implementation of a provision of the Federal Housing Enterprises Financial Safety and Soundness Act of 1992 until April 28. Some of the Biden team for the second half is still going through the senate confirmation process. Jared Bernstein's confirmation hearing is Tuesday April 18. He has previously talked about how Biden directed him to engage in housing policy discussions, how the wind-down team lost and how he was tasked with preserving the 30 year fixed rate mortgage.

Jared Bernstein also talks about the key to housing finance reform in his blog:

The key, then, is to a) put private capital in a "first loss" position ahead of the government, and b) set a price for the government insurance that accurately reflects and offsets the expected taxpayer costs of the backstop, something the GSEs decidedly did not do.

One way to interpret Bernstein's comment is to enable the companies to raise third party capital which will be private capital taking the first loss position and then restructure the remaining PSPA commitment terms so that the companies pay for it via the periodic commitment fee.

Comments on the proposed updates for the ERCF for commingled securities etc. are due May 12. The capital planning rule requires that Fannie and Freddie capital plans are submitted May 20th.

The timing is ripening for admin action. If we don't see any movement by the end of this summer, this probably isn't a problem that is going to get solved during this administration and all the benefits of solving the conservatorship problem will benefit the next president's agenda instead.

Treasury's GSE Accounting: Fully Valued With Growing Costs

From 2020-2021, the Fair Value of the GSEs stock was marked up from $108.9B to $220.9B. This enabled the Biden administration to recognize a lot more revenue from the GSEs and make more money off them:

Note 9. Investments in Government-Sponsored Enterprises

Investments in GSEs as of September 30, 2021

(In billions of dollars)	Gross Investments	Cumulative Valuation Gain/(Loss)	Fair Value
Fannie Mae senior preferred stock	158.7	(38.2)	120.5
Freddie Mac senior preferred stock	94.9	0.1	95.0
Fannie Mae warrants common stock	3.1	0.4	3.5
Freddie Mac warrants common stock	2.3	(0.4)	1.9
Total investments in GSEs	259.0	(38.1)	220.9

Investments in GSEs as of September 30, 2020

(In billions of dollars)	Gross Investments	Cumulative Valuation Gain/(Loss)	Fair Value
Fannie Mae senior preferred stock	137.8	(79.5)	58.3
Freddie Mac senior preferred stock	83.9	(46.0)	37.9
Fannie Mae warrants common stock	3.1	5.2	8.3
Freddie Mac warrants common stock	2.3	2.1	4.4
Total investments in GSEs	227.1	(118.2)	108.9

Government Investment In GSEs (Treasury Department)

From 2021-2022, the Fair Value of the GSEs stock was marked up again, but Fannie Mae was marked down, implying that the companies were marked up to full valuation:

Note 8. Investments in Government-Sponsored Enterprises

Investments in GSEs as of September 30, 2022

(In billions of dollars)	Gross Investments	Cumulative Valuation Gain/(Loss)	Fair Value
Fannie Mae senior preferred stock	177.7	(62.0)	115.7
Freddie Mac senior preferred stock	106.6	(2.1)	104.5
Fannie Mae warrants common stock	3.1	(0.9)	2.2
Freddie Mac warrants common stock	2.3	(1.0)	1.3
Total investments in GSEs	289.7	(66.0)	223.7

Investments in GSEs as of September 30, 2021

(In billions of dollars)	Gross Investments	Cumulative Valuation Gain/(Loss)	Fair Value
Fannie Mae senior preferred stock	158.7	(38.2)	120.5
Freddie Mac senior preferred stock	94.9	0.1	95.0
Fannie Mae warrants common stock	3.1	0.4	3.5
Freddie Mac warrants common stock	2.3	(0.4)	1.9
Total investments in GSEs	259.0	(38.1)	220.9

Investment in Government-Sponsored Enterprises (Treasury)

To finance these government assets, the government has debt costs. For years interest rates were low and from 2012-2019, the government took all the money from Fannie and Freddie and so the investment was profitable. Since the government stopped taking all their money, it has been making profit on them in a low cost environment by marking up the value of its stake in them on its balance sheet. Things have changed. Now the companies are marked to full valuation and will result in annual losses for the government because their equity stake cannot increase in value, does not pay dividends, and interest rates are going up.

In 2022, total national debt was $30.9T and the government paid $475B in interest payments on the national debt. This means that any asset on the government's balance sheet was profitable if it generated 1.5% return in 2022. In the case of Fannie and Freddie $220.9B * 1.5% means that it cost the government $3.3B to carry Fannie and Freddie on its balance sheet unrestructured, which was basically breakeven since the government marked them up $2.8B. That said, the tell is that Fannie Mae was marked down 2021-2022. Going forward, however, the value of the government's equity stake will not increase and funding costs will go up. According to the CBO:

Interest costs grew 35 percent last year and are projected to grow by another

35 percent in 2023.

What this means is that the government from here on out will be losing money by carrying Fannie and Freddie in their unrestructured form and not selling its equity stake in them because of their carrying costs, which are only increasing.

The government cannot just sit on assets that are not expected to appreciate when funding rates go up. This compels the government to sell its stake in order to remove the unappreciating assets that only have increasing carrying costs from its balance sheet.

Summary and Conclusion

Exit from conservatorship is happening. Timing of when is unknown. My view is that the companies are set to achieve their statutory capital requirements through retained earnings alone during the next presidential administration at which point something has to happen. As such, either Biden resolves the end of the conservatorships or the next administration resolves them. I think that the incentives are in place for Biden to resolve them and, if true, signs would start surfacing in the coming months and once those signs surface the price will no longer be in the bargain bin.

Fannie Mae and Freddie Mac have more earnings than they have ever held in their history since Mark Calabria and Steven Mnuchin began to end the cash net worth sweep in September of 2019 and the companies make more money now than pre-conservatorship since their guarantee fees have roughly doubled.

With the FHFA director being a political appointee position and Treasury's equity agreement controlling whether or not Fannie and Freddie can access third party capital and exit conservatorship, the ball is in the administration's court. According to Calabria's book, the government has been sitting on workable capital plans that get Fannie and Freddie out of conservatorship since late summer 2020. These plans can result in billions of dollars being put towards affordable housing initiatives according to CRL's Michael Calhoun. Under Biden, Sandra Thompson has required capital plans starting next month.

No longer are the companies giving their money to the government and unlike the SPSPA liquidation preference, the government's value of the warrants is not an accounting entry, it's spendable cash. The government seems to be setting up to spend this money, and soon. In his book, Calabria says that "Building capital at the companies, with an eye toward eventual release from conservatorship ... was clearly what the statute required and Congress intended." So, not only should the government follow the law and the intentions of Congress in facilitating the end of the conservatorships, but it gets the opportunity unlock a lot of spendable cash by doing so. Lastly, Sandra Thompson has carried out a lot of regulatory work since becoming

Director of FHFA to prepare Fannie and Freddie to do equity offerings to meet their capital requirements and their subsequent life outside of conservatorship.

Treasury has made a lot of money on its investment in Fannie and Freddie, but now the tables have turned and the government cannot just sit on assets that are not expected to appreciate when its funding costs are going up. Thus, Treasury's better off selling its equity stake in Fannie and Freddie. FHFA, Fannie and Freddie are all ready to help get that done. It all is waiting on Treasury.

DC Jury Decides GSE Shareholder Contracts Breached

Aug. 17, 2023 5:44 PM ET Federal Home Loan Mortgage Corporation PFD 8.375% NCM (FMCKJ) Stock, FNMAS Stock FMCC, FMCCG, FMCCH, FMCCI, FMCCK, FMCCL, FMCCM, FMCCN, FMCCO, FMCCP, FMCCS, FMCCT, FMCKI, FMCKK, FMCKL, FMCKM, FMCKN, FMCKO, FMCKP, FNMA, FNMAG, FNMAH, FNMAJ, FNMAK, FNMAM, FNMAN, FNMAP, FNMAT, FNMFM, FNMFN, FNMFO, FREJP

Summary

- Fannie Mae and Freddie Mac shareholders win legal victory as jury finds FHFA acted arbitrarily in entering into Net Worth Sweep.
- Pending equity restructuring includes warrants, common shares, junior preferred shares, and senior preferred shares.
- There are significant, follow on implications for other cases now that a jury has decided that the government breached the implied covenant of good faith.

- AndreyPopov/iStock via Getty Images

As of August 14, 2023, Fannie Mae (OTCQB:FNMA) and Freddie Mac (OTCQB:FMCC) shareholders have a new legal victory to celebrate. After a decade of uphill legal battles, shareholders have finally notched a win, but the potential impact to outcome is much more significant than the monetary damages awarded by the jury which decided:

FHFA, in its role as the Conservator of Fannie Mae and Freddie Mac, acted arbitrarily or unreasonably in entering into the Net Worth Sweep, thereby violating the reasonable expectations of holders of Fannie Mae junior preferred stock, Freddie Mac junior preferred stock, and/or Freddie Mac common stock

Question No. 1:

Did the Plaintiffs prove by a preponderance of the evidence that FHFA, in its role as the Conservator of Fannie Mae and Freddie Mac, acted arbitrarily or unreasonably in entering into the Net Worth Sweep, thereby violating the reasonable expectations of holders of Fannie Mae junior preferred stock, Freddie Mac junior preferred stock, and/or Freddie Mac common stock?

- Fannie Mae junior preferred stock: Yes ✓ No ___
- Freddie Mac junior preferred stock: Yes ✓ No ___
- Freddie Mac common stock: Yes ✓ No ___

Question #1 Verdict (glenbradford.com)

Fannie and Freddie have been retaining earnings since 2019. Fannie and Freddie have more net worth than ever before in history since their guarantee fees have roughly doubled during conservatorship. There are four components to their pending equity restructuring:

1. Warrants (Government Owned).
2. Common Shares.
3. Junior Preferred Shares.
4. Senior Preferred Shares (Government Owned).

I only recommend owning junior preferred shares because they have dilution protection in an administrative reform outcome and the strongest legal claims in a court-led outcome.

Investment Thesis

This either gets resolved via administrative action or court action. This marks the first major FHFA loss in court where a jury unanimously decided that FHFA breached the implied covenant of good faith built into the contract rights of shareholders.

Outside of administrative reform, courts will resolve this. This jury awarded damages of $611M to shareholders. Judge Lamberth did not let plaintiffs present the expectancy reliance damage model which would have opened the door to damages closer to the outstanding par value of junior preferred, $34B+. Nearly every available damage model is designed to pay out face value to preferred shareholders, expectancy, restitution, reliance, etc. The damage model that went to trial is extremely controversial. FHFA has 60 days from the verdict to file notice of appeal. If I was Arnold and Porter I would be recommending to their client that if they wanted to proactively end the conservatorship now would be a good time to do so. Should they pursue appeal and go the court route, they risk facing a damage model that actually fits the breach of contract that a jury has decided they committed.

This court ruling in my view only helps the case for administrative reform. In an administrative solution, since the companies are retaining earnings --- receivership is off the table and junior preferred would be made whole in the process. The companies would likely turn on junior preferred dividends to settle the pending litigation while they move forward with recapitalization and release. Junior preferred would trade up to face value.

Fannie Mae Q2 2023

Fannie Mae made $5B in Q2 2023. The SPS liquidation preference was $185B and the net worth was $69B. Fannie Mae CEO Priscilla Almodovar declared Fannie Mae has been transformed on the quarterly call:

You know, this fall marks 15 years since Fannie Mae was placed in conservatorship. A lot has changed since that time. Today, Fannie Mae has been transformed. Fannie Mae is safer and stronger, thanks to years of work to improve the resiliency of our business and our steadfast focus on strong risk management. Because of this, we continue to be a stabilizing force in the market and to deliver on our mission, like we did through the COVID-19 pandemic, and how we're doing now through this challenging economic cycle. We are committed to being a reliable source of liquidity and stability to the housing finance system in the United States.

Fannie Mae has more money than they ever have had in history and the government still has them in conservatorship.

Freddie Mac Q2 2023

Freddie Mac made $2.9B in Q2 2023. The SPS liquidation preference was $111B and the net worth was $42B.

Freddie Mac has more money than they ever have had in history and the government still has them in conservatorship.

Shareholder Attorney Provides Context On Size of $611M Legal Win

The lead attorney for the shareholders compares the $611M legal victory to the $32B that shareholders invested as reported by National Mortgage Professional:

The government deserved and would have received, without the net worth sweep, a huge profit on its investment. But it was not entitled to 100% of all profits forever. That was not the deal made in September 2008. Private preferred shareholders invested over $32 billion, of which $20 billion was at the behest of government regulators during the housing crisis years of 2007 and 2008.

If FHFA allows this verdict to be appealed, it risks losing an upsized reliance damage model of $32B when it is in a position to resolve this now for much less. This puts FHFA is in a unique position to cap their litigation losses before they potentially balloon. They have about 60 days to appeal or pursue other options.

2023 Stress Tests

August 10th, FHFA released the 2023 Dodd-Frank Act Stress Test Results. The stress test results result in Fannie and Freddie making a combined $9.9B even if equity prices fall by 45% and home prices decline 38%. Under these conditions, FHFA does forecast that if they are able to use their discretionary accounting authority to write down Fannie and Freddie's assets like they did in 2008, the companies would lose $8.4B. Even with the loss the companies on a combined basis since they have been able to retain earnings since 2019 would have a net worth of $88.9B in this worst case scenario.

My perspective is that guarantee fees doubled during conservatorship and it is much harder to drain a bathtub when you pour in water as fast as it drains out, which is basically what happens to achieve these stress test results whereas in the past earnings were half what they were today and you could accumulate a few years of losses --- now even if the economy falls apart Fannie and Freddie stay afloat on earnings alone.

Meanwhile, FHFA currently has a Capital Framework which says they are undercapitalized and holds them hostage in conservatorship, but it looks like they are trying to do something about it.

FHFA put out an RFI and the intellectually honest submissions (I was able to find one exception by the guy who signed the net worth sweep that a jury ruled to be a breach of contract) all seem to call for a reworking of the ERCF which makes sense in the context of these stress test results. I walk through a handful of these submissions below and the growing chorus for admin reform now supported by this legal ruling.

FHFA's RFI On GSE Single Family Mortgage Pricing Framework

In May 2023, FHFA put out a request for input for Fannie Mae and Freddie Mac Single-Family Mortgage Pricing Framework. The basic purpose of this RFI is to solicit industry feedback on how it should match pricing up with the capital requirements imposed by the Enterprise Regulatory Capital Framework - ERCF. The industry has responded with comments and feedback. The overwhelming response to the FHFA RFI has been to streamline the capital rule and step aside.

Urban Institute

The most notable shift in my opinion coming from this RFI is the more administrative reform positioning coming from Urban Institute. Urban Institute has really evolved their perspective to be more supportive of a utility model and raising new third-party capital which is a positive shift in support of administrative reform. Urban Institute forecasts a need for Fannie and Freddie to raise private capital:

In either case, they will need to raise private capital, which will require a return attractive enough for whichever of the two models is chosen.

Urban Institute says that the ECRF needs to be revised lower:

The GSEs' approach to pricing strikes us as reasonable, but it suffers from a capital framework unnecessarily tethered to the Basel framework. The risk-invariant components and complexity of that framework are arguably appropriate for large banks, given the number and complexity of the risks they manage, but they make little sense for Fannie Mac and Freddie Mac. Applied to the GSEs, they exert unnecessary upward pressure on pricing, pressure that has been borne by the GSEs thus far but, at some point, will be passed along to the consumer. Before that happens, the FHFA should revise the requirements, removing a headwind to homeownership and better aligning the GSEs' pricing with their risk.

Lower capital requirements and raise new third-party capital is the path forward according to Urban Institute.

Community Home Lenders of America

The CHLA argues in its letter that the objective of the capital rule is for Fannie and Freddie to exit from conservatorship:

Second, while CHLA supports a key underlying objective of that capital rule - the exit of Fannie Mae and Freddie Mac from conservatorship - given the current political realities, such exit appears to be a remote, if not non-existent, possibility. In an ideal world, we would either roll back excessive fee hikes to raise capital or move forward to exit from conservatorship. Instead, arguably, we have the worst of both worlds.

The CHLA seems to think that the Biden administration is unwilling to let Fannie and Freddie recap and release and exit from conservatorship. Note that they may have submitted this letter before the legal ruling came out.

After the legal ruling came out, Rob Zimmer said that this legal ruling cements the future of Fannie and Freddie being recapped and released despite not knowing the exact timing of when:

> **Rob Zimmer** @RobTVDC · 58m
> For some time there's only been one obvious outcome for @FannieMae & @FreddieMac , and while we don't know the exact timing of when they will be recapped and released, this jury decision certainly solidifies the already-extant political consensus. 1/2
>
> ○ 3   ↺ 15   ♥ 23   ᴵᴵᴵ 599   ⬆
>
> **Rob Zimmer** @RobTVDC · 58m
> Smart financial analysts & policymakers always knew the NWS was a flawed and failed policy, and yesterday the jury agreed.
>
> Community IMBs, banks, credit unions, large homebuilders, & consumer & civil rights orgs have always thought the NWS was ill-advised, for many reasons. 2/2
>
> ○ 1   ↺ 9   ♥ 18   ᴵᴵᴵ 295   ⬆

Rob says this legal ruling cements R&R (Twitter)

Rob Zimmer seems to have reviewed the bulk of the responses to RFI etc. Rob's comments align with CHLA's Scott Olson's from last year too:

My personal opinion is that the best approach is for Fannie and Freddie to exit conservatorship under a true utility model using the housing mission tools of HERA, a vigilant FHFA that makes sure the GSEs do not take on dangerous levels of risk to maximize shareholder profit, and an explicit federal backstop to establish MBS investor confidence.

CHLA is very supportive of administrative recap and release and believes it is an eventuality --- just a matter of when.

Mortgage Bankers Association

The Mortgage Bankers Association is telling FHFA that the ERCF shouldn't be based on Basel III. Fannie and Freddie are not banks! They should have a simple capital requirement that is based on actual risk. This reads like a nudge to lower the capital requirements. Seems like there is consensus from most interested parties on this topic:

Enterprise Single-Family Pricing Framework Request for Input
August 14, 2023

focus on. The level of compatibility between the ERCF and Basel III is not clear. Revising the ERCF post-Basel III finalization will give FHFA the opportunity to address compatibility, provide transparency, and lower complexity, which will allow the Enterprises to more accurately and effectively determine capital requirements based on actual risk. This is especially important given the link between the ERCF and decisions regarding single-family pricing for the Enterprises.

* * *

MBA appreciates the opportunity to comment on the Enterprise Single-Family Pricing Framework RFI, and we urge FHFA to continue engagement with the mortgage industry to improve clarity and transparency regarding the Enterprises' pricing framework. We look forward to our continued partnership and will work closely with you in the coming months on this and other critical housing finance issues.

Sincerely,

Robert D. Broeksmit, CMB
President and Chief Executive Officer
Mortgage Bankers Association

MBA RFI Feedback Ending (FHFA)

Prior CEO of MBA David H Stevens declares this court ruling a landmark win for GSE Shareholder interests and had this to say on HousingWire:

The victory in Berkley vs. FHFA is sweet for shareholders, notably in that it's their first one since the beginning of conservatorship, said David Stevens, a former Federal Housing Administration commissioner and Mortgage Bankers Association president.

"Whether this sets the tone for a new direction for the conservatorship is yet to be seen," Stevens said. "But without question, a political leadership that oversees these two companies in Washington will be likely focusing on options ahead. While the jury awarded less than what was asked for by the plaintiffs, it is without question victory for the shareholder interest. What happens next will be interesting."

David H Stevens has come full circle this year as he is advocating for administrative reform to end the conservatorships of Fannie and Freddie as a means of solving their political problem brought on by making the FHFA director a political appointee thanks to the SCOTUS ruling in Collins vs. Yellen.

Center for Responsible Lending

The CRL has replied, arguing that the ERCF needs to be considered and recalibrated to take into consideration the actual financial risks of Fannie and Freddie:

The case for reconsidering the Enterprise Regulatory Capital Framework ("ERCF") is clear and compelling.

...

Developments over the past two and a half years have made it even clearer that the ERCF is seriously flawed.

...

The ERCF stands as an obstacle to progress on these fronts. Given the stress test results, the developments since the adoption of the ERCF that have reduced the GSEs risks, and the multiple fallacies of the ERCF itself, FHFA should reconsider the amount of capital required by the ERCF and the ERCF's definition of what constitutes capital.

...

And, so long as the GSEs are expected to achieve a "reasonable rate of return" on an unreasonably large capital base-currently over $300 billion- it will be difficult, if not impossible, for the GSEs to pursue such initiatives at the scale needed to fulfill their mission.

Independent Community Bankers of America

The ICBA has replied calling for FHFA to work with the U.S. Treasury to restructure its ownership stake in Fannie and Freddie in order to attract:

ICBA therefore strongly urges the FHFA to establish a revised single-family pricing framework alongside a roadmap for the Enterprises to raise outside equity, eventually exit conservatorship, and to do so with a clear vision of their ongoing role in the secondary housing market.

...

Absent any changes to the preferred stock purchasing agreements (PSPAs), this means that they will then be required to resume sweeping any excess earnings to the Treasury, effectively making it impossible to exit conservatorship. ICBA has long argued that a perpetual conservatorship is unacceptable and unsustainable.

...

Without acknowledging that the GSEs need to prepare to exit conservatorship, there is little incentive to materially change to ROE to a rate that would make them competitive for investor funding as semi-private companies. This concern is exacerbated by the fact that the GSEs remain undercapitalized according to the existing ECRF and that the government's ownership of the Enterprises remains unresolved. As mandated by the Housing and Economic Recovery Act (HERA), FHFA must therefore collaborate with the U.S. Treasury to begin the process of resolving the government's ownership of Fannie Mae and Freddie Mac.

After nearly fifteen years of conservatorship, ICBA is greatly concerned that the lack of progress in resolving this issue by FHFA and the Treasury endangers the safety and soundness of both Enterprises and could pose a threat to the stability of the mortgage market.

The ICBA call for Treasury to work with FHFA to resolve its equity interests in Fannie and Freddie aligns with charting their path out of conservatorship.

NAFCU

NAFCU provided a comment letter which speaks for itself:

Until the FHFA can articulate its expectations for returns while supporting high capitalization and low rates, the FHFA should not control guarantee fees for the GSEs. NAFCU supports allowing the GSEs to ultimately be removed from their conservatorships and recognizes that goal would be delayed by substandard returns.

The GSEs need to make returns that support their capital requirements according to NAFCU in order to ultimately exit conservatorship.

National Association of Realtors

NAR targets ROE based on utilities:

Furthermore, the FHFA should formally adopt a return on equity (ROE) appropriate for market utilities, implement a cap and floor on ROE, explore an explicit government guarantee, and must establish a robust and durable process for establishing appropriate returns at the Enterprises during conservatorship and after.

NAR also focuses on life after conservatorship:

The FHFA should continue its important work to develop a process that sets a band of returns for the Enterprises' cost of capital to use in establishing their g-fees and pricing outside of conservatorship.

NAR also says that the capital required by the ECRF is excessive:

These implied ROEs are appropriate to the Enterprises but were achieved for the wrong reason; the level of capital in ECRF is excessive.

If the FHFA adjusts the ECRF so that the companies can hold less capital than their current ECRF, then NAR will be happy.

Housing Policy Council

This letter is signed by Ed Demarco, the guy who signed the net worth sweep that the jury just ruled to be a breach of contract and was submitted the same day the jury ruled that his actions breached the shareholder contracts.

Ed Demarco argues that the Basel III Proposal Conflicts with the FHFA ERCF. Further, he ***notably*** recommends increasing guarantee fees to support the ERCF. I couldn't find any other comment letter where someone else is arguing for increased fees like Ed Demarco of the Housing Policy Council appears to be:

The FHFA commentary on the recent pricing changes focus in part on the need to generate sufficient returns to satisfy the capital standards set forth in the Enterprise Regulatory Capital Framework (ERCF). HPC is on record supporting the ERCF, recognizing that small adjustments may be necessary. The current framework reflects the substantial research and analysis performed by FHFA and the Enterprises as well as extensive commentary from stakeholders. The existing ERCF was promulgated following a full comment period, which provided the opportunity for meaningful input from all sectors of the mortgage industry. No standard will ever fully satisfy every housing stakeholder, but this ERCF represents a well-developed compromise. We recommend that FHFA retain the ERCF *and require pricing levels that will allow the Enterprises to earn* FHFA's targeted rate of return in accordance with the ERCF, over a reasonable period of time.

Leave it to Ed Demarco to argue for additional increases to guarantee fees that completely ignore the recent stress test results and the doubling of guarantee fees during conservatorship. His perspective seems to have fallen out of step with Urban Institute.

Breach of Contract Damage Models

If you have not been closely following the developments, it is worth noting that Judge Lamberth rejected all four damage models presented by the plaintiffs - namely, expectancy, restitution, reliance, and the lost share alternative - prior to the trial. The plaintiffs are now seeking to appeal these decisions with the aim of obtaining a damage model that aligns more closely with their actual financial loss due to the net worth sweep.

During the trial, Judge Lamberth allowed one specific damage model to proceed, resulting in a relatively modest damages amount of $611 million. However, this outcome has stirred controversy due to the nature of breach of contract damages models, which are designed to restore the injured party to their pre-breach state. In the context of junior preferred shares, this would involve receiving a payout close to the face value. While the plaintiffs achieved a favorable outcome in the trial, the damages awarded were notably smaller than what one would anticipate in a breach of contract case, where the typical outcome is closer to a payout that would be closer to the original value of the contract, or "par." I've heard estimates anywhere between 8-18 months for the duration of such an appeal.

Expectancy

The concept of "Expectancy" entails restoring the non-breaching party to the state they would have been in had the breach not occurred. This involves considering the repayment of the liquidation preference that would have been received and factoring in the principal amount along with pre-judgment interest at a rate of 6%, approximately equaling 150% of the principal.

Restitution

"Restitution," on the other hand, centers around ensuring that the breaching party returns any net benefits acquired through the contract. This involves deducting any gains obtained by the non-breaching party as a result of the contract.

Reliance

The principle of "Reliance" seeks to reinstate the plaintiff parties to the position they were in prior to entering into the contract.

The reliance damages model were in my view incorrectly not addressed by this Jury because Lamberth prevented them from going to trial twice due to timing issues, not because they were not a valid damages model.

CapWealth's Pagliara on American Banker

In response to this ruling, some have speculated that FHFA will appeal, but FHFA said they will review and determine post-trial options according to American Banker:

"FHFA, Fannie Mae and Freddie Mac are disappointed in the verdict," an agency spokesman wrote in an email to American Banker. "FHFA will review the verdict and determine post-trial options."

In fact, GSE Shareholder Tim Pagliara says not so fast:

But a move to challenge the verdict would not be a risk-free proposition for the FHFA, Tim Pagliara, chief investment officer of the financial advisory firm CapWealth, said.

"If the government appeals the verdict, it could backfire and the $612 million verdict could balloon to over $30 billion because the government could be forced to pay 100% of the preferred stock that they breached the contract on," Pagliara, whose clients are GSE shareholders, said. "There is controversy surrounding the damage model that the jury was allowed to consider in the trial that was just completed."

I believe Tim Pagliara is referring to the reliance damages model that Lamberth prevented from going to trial twice which effectively equals par less cumulative dividends.

Tyler vs. Hennepin

GSE Shareholder Plaintiff Bryndon Fisher points to Tyler vs. Hennepin as a means to try and get his case heard in the federal circuit arguing that his case was wrongly decided and this new Supreme Court ruling changes everything.

I applaud Bryndon Fisher's legal efforts. Below is the overall most recent litigation calendar from the end of last month:

GSEs - Litigation Calendar

2023			
Jul	Aug	Sep	Q4
[1] Trial *(7/24/23 - 8/4/23)* Trial Verdict Expected *(~8/7/23)*			
[2] Oral Arguments *(~9/4/23)* Decision Expected *(~Q4 '23)*			
[3] District Court Remand Schedule *(7/12/23)*			
[4] Oral Arguments *(~Q3 23)* Decision Expected *(~Q4 '23)*			
[5] Oral Arguments *(~Q3 23)* Decision Expected *(~Q4 '23)*			
[6] En Banc Petition(s) *(~Q4 '23)*			

[1] *Consolidated v. FHFA/GSEs (Claim: Contracts implied covenant)*
[2] *Collins v. Yellen (Claim: Removal provision remedy + Appropriations clause)*
[3] *Rop v. FHFA (Claim: Removal provision remedy)*
[4] *Bhatti v. FHFA (Claim: Removal provision remedy)*
[5] *Kelly v. US (Claim: Takings + JPS Contracts)*
[6] *COFC: Wazee + Fisher (Claim: Takings + Unjust Enrichment)*

July Litigation Calendar (Twitter)

You will note that Oral arguments in Collins vs. Yellen are early next month.

Risks

Fannie and Freddie shareholders could continue to lose all the lawsuits and the government could keep them in conservatorship despite eventually retaining enough earnings to be adequately capitalized. The world could fall apart and become unrecognizable with more devastating economic consequences than outlined in the 2023 Stress Test and the companies could be placed into receivership where existing shareholders are zeroed out. Common shares could be diluted out of any material upside in any equity restructuring.

I think the biggest risk is really one of time. I've been in this trade since 2014. I thought that this would get resolved by the original Lamberth ruling that went completely opposite to my interpretation of the law. What is ironic is that the day before the 8 Jury members unanimously decided FHFA breached the contracts, they requested to have the law provided to them so they could read it for themselves. It is nice to see a panel of 8 Americans read the law and interpret it the same way I have in a world where no court seems to agree with prior FHFA director Mark Calabria's interpretation of the law.

Summary and Conclusion

The current Biden administration has been silent on the issue for restructuring its equity position in Fannie and Freddie but I suspect that will not be the case during the rest of the Biden admin and I believe that this jury verdict opens up a path for moving forward with an administrative initiative to release Fannie and Freddie from conservatorship. The overwhelming response to FHFA's RFI has been to set the ECRF to be more in line with current guarantee fees in a post-conservatorship environment and to solicit input from US Treasury. I found a family office note that summarizes the impact of this legal ruling nicely:

> Congratulations to Hamish Hume and the entire Plaintiffs prosecution team, and most importantly the shareholders that stood up, fought, and spent millions of dollars fighting a government that prints money to betray its own citizens. The significance of what happened is not in the damage award $612,000,000 (the only appealable part of the judgment- very controversial) but the fact that a jury of 8 found that the government acted in bad faith in dealing with Billions of dollars of shareholders interests. There are significant, follow on implications for other cases. We think the Pfds double from here by year-end. Keep in mind, the GSE's passed the 2023 stress test with a 9 billion profit. After doubling down with an embedded 38% drop in housing prices nationwide. They are now among the strongest financial services firms in the world." - Family Office CIO

Family Office CIO Note (Twitter)

I recommend junior preferred shares because in any equity restructuring that happens outside of receivership they are made whole in addition to having strong enough legal claims now that they have won breach of contract to have a path forward of seeing par under a reliance damages model.

White House And Treasury Can Solve Affordability Crisis With GSEs

Summary
- Fannie Mae and Freddie Mac are still in conservatorship despite their record-high net worth and profitability.
- There is a path to accessing funds to solve the affordable housing crisis.
- The Biden administration has the opportunity to secure a future of equal opportunity affordable housing, and there is a sense of urgency.

Fannie Mae (OTCQB:FNMA) and Freddie Mac (OTCQB:FMCC) are two companies still in conservatorship despite making more money than ever before and having more net worth than ever before. It can be argued that:

1. There is an affordable housing crisis.
2. The companies have been reformed.
3. There is a path to accessing $100B to solve the affordable housing crisis.
4. There is a sense of urgency.

The Biden administration can lock in its future of housing finance reform and allocate the $100B if it wants to, but it would have to start moving quickly with direction from the White House or the US Treasury.

Gary Hindes standing next to Vice President Biden in New York.
(Gary Hindes standing next to Vice President Biden in New York.)

Fannie and Freddie shareholder Gary Hindes wants to know "When do we get our companies back?" Gary Hindes led Delaware's Democratic party, helping Joe Biden build a prodigious network beyond its narrow borders. So far, the Biden administration has been unresponsive toward any restructuring initiatives or requests. In about a year we will have a general election and President Trump is leading in the polls. Previously Trump wrote a letter saying that he would end the conservatorships if he had a year or two more time without an Obama-era official incumbent that he could not fire. If the Biden administration does not take action, eventually a Republican administration will release Fannie and Freddie and implement their policy objectives in the process and likely void a lot of Biden's policy objectives that Biden could have locked in, a potentially easily missed opportunity to secure a future of equal opportunity affordable housing.

Investment Thesis

As Gary Hindes points out, Fannie and Freddie's combined net worths are at record highs and they returned to profitability over a decade ago. On August 14, a jury ruled that the government acted in bad faith when it imposed the Net Worth Sweep. Lawyers representing plaintiffs and the government will be posting a joint motion for calculation of prejudgment interest on Friday. Then, we can expect Lamberth to enter a final judgment for the shareholder plaintiffs against the government. Junior preferred shares currently trade at less than 10 cents on the dollar despite the only possibility of them being zeroed out or impaired (receivership) being well off the table noting prior CEO of Freddie Mac Don Layton's comments that "Given the existing level of capital at the two companies, the probability of taxpayers having to inject more funds into the GSEs is approaching levels that I believe are so small they cannot be statistically measured." In any recap and release, if junior preferred refuses any conversion offer, dividends would eventually resume when common dividends resume and junior preferred would appreciate closer to or above par value depending on the series.

Is Conservatorship Undermining Established Solvency Law?

Prior FHFA director Mark Calabria got hired on to lead FHFA where he stopped the cash payments from Fannie and Freddie to Treasury after he wrote a paper "The Conservatorships of Fannie and Freddie Mac: Actions Violate HERA and Established Insolvency Principles".

Investment titan Bruce Berkowitz this past month gave an interview on WealthTrack saying that his experience with the government's handling of Fannie and Freddie now makes him:

more hesitant to deal with highly regulated businesses where one civil servant can decide whether a very large company lives or dies based upon a perception of social good and without any respect for owners.

In fact, the Fannie Mae and Freddie Mac situation made me think that ownership is becoming an illusion in highly regulated companies.

Jury Verdict Pending Lamberth Judgment

On August 14, a jury ruled that FHFA violated reasonable expectations when arranging the net worth sweep:

> Question No. 1:
>
> Did the Plaintiffs prove by a preponderance of the evidence that FHFA, in its role as the Conservator of Fannie Mae and Freddie Mac, acted arbitrarily or unreasonably in entering into the Net Worth Sweep, thereby violating the reasonable expectations of holders of Fannie Mae junior preferred stock, Freddie Mac junior preferred stock, and/or Freddie Mac common stock?
>
> - Fannie Mae junior preferred stock: Yes ✓ No ___
> - Freddie Mac junior preferred stock: Yes ✓ No ___
> - Freddie Mac common stock: Yes ✓ No ___

Jury Decision Lamberth 2023 Verdict (Jury Decision Lamberth 2023 Verdict)

Lamberth has not yet issued a judgment on this. Judgment in favor of plaintiffs is expected later this year.

Stress Tests Reveal Reformed GSEs

Gary Hindes points out in his letter that even if there was a 38% housing price decline that Fannie and Freddie would earn $9.9B according to their stress tests. He argues that after 16 years of conservatorship and all-time highs in shareholder equity this last quarter there simply is no legitimate reason to keep these companies in conservatorship any longer.

FHFA Annual Performance Plan for FY 2024

The number 1 strategic goal jives with being adequately capitalized outside of conservatorship:

- Strategic Goal 1: Secure the regulated entities' safety and soundness

The only potential blocker I foresee to achieving this goal may be addressed by this Annual Performance plan, possibly as soon as this year:

- 1.3.3 | Issue a final rule enhancing the Enterprise Regulatory Capital Framework (ERCF) | Target: December 31, 2023
- Measure 1.3.3 - FHFA will publish a final rule amending the ERCF to address guarantees on commingled securities, multifamily loans secured by properties with a government subsidy, derivatives and cleared transactions, and to make other enhancements. The final rule will be published in the Federal Register and on FHFA's website.

This final rule may address the disconnect between the ERCF and G-fees that would address the issue of commercially reasonable returns. Earlier this year, FHFA pointed out:

The Enterprises are in the process of phasing in the effects of the ERCF by gradually increasing returns over time to help ensure that they achieve commercially reasonable returns

This final rule may address the responses to the RFI with respect to the following two questions:

1. What is an appropriate long-term commercially reasonable return on capital threshold for the Enterprises to achieve?
2. Should risk-based pricing be calibrated to the ERCF?

Calabria originally forecasted IPOs in 2021, so I am not sure if these questions mentioned above are that important to reprivatizing Fannie and Freddie, I just take an interest in the back and forth here.

FHFA 2023 PAR

FHFA issued its FY 2023 Performance and Accountability Report on November 8. I have bolded the part that I want to emphasize:

FHFA continues to strengthen the safety and soundness of its regulated entities. In March 2023, FHFA published a notice of proposed rulemaking to further enhance the Enterprise Regulatory Capital Framework (ERCF) that would implement the lessons learned through the continued application of the ERCF, adopted in FY 2021, **and better reflect the risks inherent in the Enterprises' business models**. FHFA also issued guidance, such as Advisory Bulletin 2023-03 on model risk management, to address and set expectations for the regulated entities' business practices

...

In May 2023, FHFA also published a request for input (RFI) on the Enterprises' single-family pricing framework to gather further feedback regarding the goals and policy priorities FHFA should pursue in its oversight of this framework. Together, these steps will strengthen safety and soundness, better ensure the Enterprises fulfill their statutory missions, and more accurately align pricing with the expected financial performance and risks of the underlying loans.

It looks like the FHFA is looking to align risk with pricing to me as part of this final rule amending the ERCF in the next month and a half. As an aside, it looks like FHFA has not met their stated goal as follows:

1.3.1: Provide decision to Enterprises regarding completeness of resolution plan submissions in conjunction with readiness activities | July 31, 2023 | NOT MET

They probably want to have resolution plans in place before moving forward with letting Fannie and Freddie chart their path out of conservatorship. Be not worried for FHFA's 2024 plan has this target for December 31, 2023:

1.3.2 | Assess the resolution plan submissions against applicable regulatory standards and requirements | December 31, 2023

This is shaping up for an interesting end of year 2023.

Enterprise Regulatory Capital Framework

FHFA spoke to the annual capital plans in this section:

Finally, FHFA implemented requirements that each Enterprise submit annual capital plans to FHFA and provide prior notice for certain capital actions. The capital planning requirements allow the Enterprises to identify the amount of capital they need to raise to meet the requirements in the Enterprise Regulatory Capital Framework and to consider the timing of when to raise capital and what types of capital to raise. The amendments help provide a stable regulatory capital framework for the Enterprises as they continue to build capital, as well as after they achieve adequate capitalization under the Enterprise Regulatory Capital Framework.

Note that it is impossible for this capital planning rule to have any practical application with the SPSPA currently laying siege to the companies' earnings and their balance sheets with terms that crowd out any chance of attracting third-party capital as hypothecated by the executed US Treasury agreement with Fannie Mae and Freddie Mac.

Thoughts On Timing

Prior White House National Economic Council Director Brian Deese posted a month ago that "We need more active fiscal policy on housing. We need to incentivize the building of affordable housing. We should do that now, and not admire the problem in 2025,25,27." His replacement, Lael Brainard, is scheduled to speak on December 7 at the National Press Club with FHFA's Sandra Thompson. The 2023 Solutions For Affordable Housing's event posts a focus of:

Our focus is on housing priorities that are tangible, impactful, and achievable.

It is hard for me to imagine that such an event could be held with the head of the WH and the head of the FHFA both speaking where a solution that addresses the affordable housing crisis ignores the potential combination attack of government spending of $100B plus locking in of future administrative priorities.

Summary and Conclusion

The companies' 16,000 employees of these public companies and their thousands of shareholders want to at least know what the reason is for the continued conservatorship at this point where:

1. The companies have more net worth than ever before in history.
2. The companies have been profitable for over a decade.
3. The companies will be profitable during a 38% housing price decline.
4. A jury ruled the government acted in bad faith when arranging the NWS to prevent the companies from exiting conservatorship.
5. The administration that lets them out of conservatorship gets to lock in their policies for future administrations.
6. The government is no longer incentivized to keep them in conservatorship. In fact, financially they are incentivized to end the conservatorships.
7. The administration that lets them out can allocate ~$100B.

Shares of Fannie and Freddie junior preferred stock trade at less than 10 cents on the dollar -- which indicates that people have given up on the Biden administration's ability to make a rational decision and a series of Democrat-only presidencies are similarly situated for the foreseeable future.

White House And Treasury Housing Leadership Should End GSE Conservatorships

Summary
- Fannie Mae and Freddie Mac have been retaining earnings since 2019 on their path out of conservatorship.
- The government has been sued by investors for imposing the net worth sweep, but courts have mostly ruled in favor of the government.
- The White House, FHFA, and Treasury are now engaged in discussions about increasing housing supply and potentially ending the conservatorships.

Chip Somodevilla/Getty Images News

Fannie Mae (OTCQB:FNMA) and Freddie Mac (OTCQB:FMCC) are two companies that were placed into conservatorship in 2008. Since 2019 they have been retaining earnings on their path out of conservatorship. Investors have sued the government for imposing the net worth sweep saying that it was a takings and that it was illegal. The courts have ruled that the government can do whatever it wants and that it isn't a takings if they take everything for nothing -- because the law is written to enable FHFA to act in its own best interests. There are still two valuable pieces of pending litigation, the ROP case and the class action case where a jury ruled that the government breached the contracts of shareholders. The rulings so far, however, continue to leave the outcome here to administrative action.

Investment Thesis

Ending the conservatorships of Fannie and Freddie, according to the government's CBO report would put junior preferred stockholders in a position to be made whole. The $100B of warrant proceeds from the CBO report could then be allocated across the 435 congressional districts or $230M per congressional district to address local affordable housing initiatives nationwide. Since the Supreme Court ruled that FHFA is a political appointee position, continued conservatorship leaves their current policies unprotected from the next FHFA director from using its endless powers as conservator to change everything around. Thus, the Supreme Court ruling makes continued conservatorship more risky than ending the conservatorships. Administrative action can be taken by any presidential administration to restructure Treasury's equity stake and end the conservatorships. Treasury already has an agreement in place with the companies to do just this that it entered into in 2021 but has not yet been implemented as the companies continue to retain capital.

White House Is Engaged

The Director of the National Economic Council Lael Brainard spoke at a housing symposium on December 7. This is notable in its own right because this is the first time she publicly talked about housing. In her prepared remarks I found two interesting snippets:

Our first major priority is increasing the supply of affordably priced homes in order to lower housing costs. We are using every lever at our disposal - legislative proposals, **our administrative authorities**, our convening power, and our bully pulpit - to do so.

But **we cannot wait for Congress to act**. Through our Housing Supply Action Plan, we are reducing barriers to housing and offering new and improved financing for affordable housing development.

Housing Supply Action Plan

When you look at the Housing Supply Action Plan, it was announced in May 2022 to close the Housing Supply gap in 5 years. Although there are no explicit references to Fannie and Freddie, this plan was released a month after FHFA released its strategic 5-year plan for FY 2022-2026. Executing objective 1.3.3 ends the conservatorships:

Oversee the Enterprises' implementation of capital plans to achieve regulatory capital requirements

2021 Fact Sheet

The Housing Supply Action Plan is based on a September 2021 fact sheet where Biden says they will do everything they can to produce more affordable housing:

President Biden is **committed to using every tool available in government to produce more affordable housing supply as quickly as possible**, and to make supply available to families in need of affordable, quality housing - rather than to large investors.

This fact sheet addresses learning and listening sessions:

Launching Learning and Listening Sessions with Local Leaders: The persistent imbalances in the U.S. housing market have formed over many decades and it will take concerted effort and iterative policymaking to correct them. To this end, the White House, HUD, and FHFA will convene state and local officials and stakeholders for a series of peer learning and listening sessions. These sessions will allow for the exchange of best practices on locally led zoning reform to address supply and affordability challenges, including a virtual session on accessory dwelling units hosted by FHFA in September. **The sessions will also identify the obstacles to implementation that** remain, which the President's Build Back Better Agenda and potentially **federal administrative action, can help address.**

One such listening session was held in Franklin TN in October of this year.

FHFA's Sandra Thompson flew to Franklin TN to talk workforce housing in October. There she learned about how administrative action can help solve the affordable housing crisis. The Mayor of Franklin Ken Moore said this, "We are confident that Director Thompson will take these ideas and lead at a national level to enhance sustainable communities where everyone can live and work."

FHFA is engaged. Now Treasury is engaged.

Treasury Is Engaged

Now Treasury is engaged. Treasury's Deputy Secretary Wally Adeyamo traveled to Georgia to talk about the importance of investments to increase housing supply:

At 7:30 AM ET, Deputy Secretary Adeyomo will convene a roundtable with financial institution leaders on **the importance of an equitable and inclusive national financial strategy**. This event is closed press.

At 1:00 PM ET, Deputy Secretary Adeyomo and Atlanta Mayor Andre

Dickens will tour Two Peachtree, a former office building that is being converted into a multi-use space that includes affordable housing units and a housing assistance center thanks to federal support for cities during the pandemic and economic recovery. Following the tour, **the Deputy Secretary and Mayor will host a roundtable to discuss the importance of investments to increase housing supply** and lower rental costs. This event is closed press.

FHFA and Treasury are now talking with local Mayors about the importance of investments to increase housing supply. The Biden administration has said before that such listening sessions would potentially lead to federal administrative action to help address obstacles to implementation.

Housing Industry Leaders Call For End of Conservatorship

The day the White House leaders spoke at Solutions 2023, David Stevens, Ted Tozer and Scott Olson published on HOUSINGWIRE that FHFA and Treasury should release the GSEs from conservatorship as soon as possible.

David Stevens directly gave me the following quote:

I think the growing call to release the GSE's warrants attention by the administration. Clearly there is increased concern about the risks of an endless array of politically motivated FHFA Directors tinkering with these important companies. Release is the only option to protect them.

In their article, they emphasize the problems with continuing conservatorship:

1. Continued conservatorship makes it harder for the GSEs themselves to focus on long-term management and housing affordability objectives.
2. Continued conservatorship makes it harder to retain talent at Fannie and Freddie as senior executives keep leaving after concluding there is no end to conservatorship in sight.
3. Continued conservatorship puts taxpayers at risk in the event of a downturn when there is broad agreement around a true utility model.

The authors argue that FHFA has a duty to end the conservatorships:

But ultimately FHFA has the authority - even a duty - under HERA to take the GSEs out of conservatorship, working with the Treasury which holds its preferred stock.

Continued conservatorships seem to undermine the administration's policy objectives stated earlier.

Prior CFO of Fannie Mae Tim Howard

Tim Howard addresses his thoughts on why the Biden administration would want to resolve the conservatorships:

As I've said often, returning the companies to their former states of shareholder-owned companies, with capital requirements that allow them to set their guaranty fees on an economic basis to the benefit of lower-income borrowers (whose share of loans guaranteed by Fannie and Freddie has plunged since the conservatorships), should be a "wheelhouse" initiative for a Democratic administration that claims to support affordable housing. And as I detailed in my current post-which was written with the administration's senior policymakers, and those who know or might influence them, in mind (and that I know has been circulated widely)-there IS in fact "An Easy Way Out" of the Fannie and Freddie conservatorships that would be a win for all stakeholders, and for which the Biden administration could take credit.

Will they embrace that way out? I wish I knew. But "kicking the can down the road" won't result in a better resolution than the one I've proposed, and it WILL result in some other administration getting the credit (and the value of Treasury's warrants for 79.9 percent of the companies' common stock) for whatever that resolution ultimately turns out to be.

The Biden admin is perfectly positioned to resolve the conservatorships and take credit.

Summary and Conclusion

White House leadership is now addressing housing. FHFA has been to local listening sessions. Treasury is engaged as well. Biden's policy objectives can be met by ending the conservatorships. Continued conservatorship undermines the administration's stated goals and objectives of closing the housing supply gap. Junior preferred shares would be made whole in any restructuring outside of receivership. Resolving the conservatorships not only helps Biden achieve housing goals by locking in his administration's policies and priorities to prevent future tinkering from subsequent FHFA directors but also achieves policy objectives by allowing the Biden admin to potentially allocate $100B of warrant proceeds to 435 congressional districts nationwide or $230M per congressional district on a local level. A research report written by Calhoun and Ranieri concludes that this path forward would help close the racial homeownership gap:

Dedicating all or a substantial share of these assets to affordable housing and racial equity would provide critically needed aid to millions of households, boost the housing and construction industry and the overall economy, and provide a means to measurably close the racial homeownership gap and the resulting wealth gap.

This would put money behind the Biden admin's conversations with local leaders and close the affordable housing supply gap. This is readily achievable and it would appear that the Biden administration is in a position to act with recent WH and Treasury activity indicating they are engaging housing industry stakeholders.

Law, Policy, And My Journey: Fannie And Freddie's Conservatorship Unveiled

Dec. 26, 2023 5:02 PM ET

Thank you for the article. We appreciate the analysis, but it looks like you just covered these tickers earlier this month (as well as last month), also with a buy rating. Per policy, please note that we're looking for contributors to present their complete analysis (which should also include a comprehensive long-term thesis) with their first article. This policy is a result of receiving reader complaints about authors who submit multiple articles within a short time frame covering the same company. Remember that articles should generally present theses that are mid-term/long-term in nature, so updating readers every few weeks, or even more than quarterly, about minor news should be reserved for the comments threads of existing articles. Please see our guidelines on follow-up articles. Much of the article also centers on backwards-looking information, as well as your personal journey. While this is very interesting and may make an excellent blog post, it doesn't really push the investment thesis for these securities forward.

Summary

The author has invested in Fannie Mae and Freddie Mac junior preferred stock and believes they are on a path to being made whole.

The prevailing legal interpretation favors the government's administrative reform steps of recapitalization and release.

The author believes that Fannie Mae and Freddie Mac will hit statutory capital requirements in the next presidential term at the latest, leading to significant gains for junior preferred stock.

SergeyNivens/iStock via Getty Images

My name is Glen Richard Bradford. My penname is G. Richard Bradford III. I have written 5+ books on Fannie and Freddie that can be found on amazon and hundreds of articles that can be found on SeekingAlpha. My grandfather's last words to me were to just help one more person when I asked him if there was anything else he wished he could have done on his death bed. For me, this article for you is one of those things.

I recently read Billy Walters' book Gambler: Secrets from a Life at Risk. I'd love for him to be able to read what I'm writing here. His experience with adverse legal rulings and things taking forever and being disappointingly wrong is relatable. If he is reading this, note Carl Icahn did buy Fannie and Freddie in 2014. Reading Billy's book and what I believe to be good timing are what is inspiring me to write this tell-all.

The purpose of this article is to potentially inspire you, the reader in at least one of a couple different possible ways and to offer some perspective that may help you navigate around some of the pitfalls that I have succumbed to and am still admittedly working my way through and clawing my way out of. This is a tell-all. All combined, this culminates into an investment thesis in Fannie Mae and Freddie Mac junior preferred stock. I originally invested in Fannie Mae (FNMA) and Freddie Mac (FMCC) common shares in the summer of 2014 before Lamberth creatively interpreted HERA to permit FHFA to do whatever it wants to as conservator, not limited to but including taking all of the money and giving it to US Treasury for no consideration. I do not believe that is the way that the law was intended to be interpreted when it was originally drafted, but I don't think that it kills this investment thesis.

Investment Thesis

Fannie and Freddie junior preferred like FNMAS and FMCKJ are on a collision course with being made whole. The companies have been retaining earnings since 2019. The prevailing legal interpretation of the law favors the administrative reform steps of recapitalization and release. A series of unfortunate events has brought this opportunity to you at levels that completely ignore the prevailing agreements and circumstances. If Biden does not resolve the conservatorships this term, Fannie Mae and Freddie Mac will hit statutory capital requirements during the next presidential term absent the SPSPA. At that point, Treasury following through with its agreements with Fannie and Freddie would end their conservatorships and make junior preferred whole. Junior preferred currently trade at around 10% of face value making them a 10-bagger in that time frame. About a month ago, the large sellers of Fannie and Freddie junior preferred were cleared out and so their prices have so far strongly reverted back to the mean, so to speak. I believe from here they will continue make significant gains in the coming months leading up to an election where the candidate leading in the polls openly favors recap and release.

FNMAS Price Chart (Stockcharts.com)

Relevant Learning Experiences From My Personal Journey

Given that my investment in Fannie and Freddie has now spanned nearly 10 years and has consumed over 100% of my net worth --- I think that telling my story about how I got here may help the reader understand where I am coming from and better judge my perspective for themselves.

Low P/E ~ More Reward and More Risk

I'm 37. When I was young, my grandfather suggested a few stocks pointing out that companies with low P/E (Price to earnings) ratios were inexpensive but they were risky. I think my first investment under his guidance was Agco, which promptly went bankrupt. My next investment was under my mom's guidance and was Genesis Health Ventures, an investment into the company that she worked for at the time. It also went bankrupt. Needless to say, I was on a roll. I had no idea what I was doing and was properly learning the hard way. At the time, I didn't really understand capital structure or real business cycle risk or what happens when companies are unable to refinance their senior obligations and that there are different kinds of bankruptcy processes or how they generally can be expected to crush existing equity shareholders.

Logic Doesn't Always Prevail

I grew up in Mishawaka, Indiana and went to college and got a BS in Industrial Engineering and a Masters of Business Administration from the Krannert school as part of the 3+2 program before they shut down their MBA program because they were losing money on it. It's too bad they gave up on it, but it was more of a management MBA program than a business MBA program and my only meeting with the dean at the time was so that she could recommend that I seek psychological counseling because my grades slipped from 4.0 to basically F+ in some of my classes as learning the efficient market hypothesis and applying it was like swallowing mouth barf. Engineering school was great because it all compiled and made sense to me because there always was a verifiable answer based on physics and logic. Business school was more like a degree in BS. Can you make up a narrative and sell it. I remember going to an MBA case competition and losing it even though the judges all said that if they were making a purchase decision they would buy from my team which gave the most practical and profitable solution, but didn't deliver it with the right level of enthusiasm and hand gestures apparently.

Growing up this way made me naive to the truths of the world. I wasn't aware how harsh and cruel it can be. I didn't understand the extent to which fraud is mainstream. I thought that the legal system was there to actually correctly interpret the law and result in the right outcome. Based on what I was taught in school, I thought our government was a system of checks and balances and fairness prevailed at least in America. This is the context of some of the beginning of my learning experiences.

My First Major Lesson In Investing

Around 2006, a church friend Doug Hall exposed me to his mathematical model of using historical quarterly revenue and earnings to linearly regress their predictability after deseasonalizing their quarterly data, calculate an r^2 coefficient and forecast into the future on a linear/semi-log and loglog basis. I used this model to start going through and quickly evaluating 100-200 companies per day from the list of total available securities on the OTCBB.

In 2008, my neighborhood friend's father who was a CPA suggested I look into Conseco and I wrote it up on Seekingalpha and I ended up making 10x my money on it. I remember at the time trying to title it, "There is no risk with Conseco" because at the time it was easily observable that the business had turned the corner despite the stock being in the toilet. My first major lesson was that at the time I only put 10% of my portfolio in it despite being incredibly confident in it and being 22 years old. At 22 --- I had a whole lifetime of earnings ahead of me. I had just figured out that I could take out loans for school (I still have school loans) that would enable me to retain some of my earnings as a GE supply chain engineer that I could invest. In that context, I should have put 100% of everything I had into it. Long story short, I learned about position sizing and how if you are going to position size you also need to position size in the context of your personalized capitalized income into the future. If I would have taken all of my money and put it in at the time, from that context my position size may have been 10-20% and I would have ended up making over a million dollars instead of around one hundred thousand. I guess maybe I learned that lesson too hard or I would probably be further along if I had put a position cap on Fannie and Freddie and instead traded around it. Not having a position limit ceiling has prohibited me from managing other people's money in the process but as you will see --- I am doing fine and if you ask me, I will be fine.

Getting Defrauded Big Time

"They can't all be fraud" was generally my investment thesis of my limited partnerships that I managed as a hedge fund manager 2009-2011. After Conseco, I was making more money trading stocks than working since I couldn't find a corporate job the summer of 2009 because of the recession after working 3 engineering co-op's at General Electric's appliance park in rotating semesters prior. I had emailed CNBC's Jim Cramer while I worked there since they had his email in the system since GE was the parent company. He replied and I started writing for TheStreet.com and James Altucher's Stockpickr.com and was getting over 100,000 reads on the articles I was writing. I even ended up writing a series for the Motley Fool where I went through and priced every company in the S&P 500 in a month or two. My edge is I could cover more ground faster than any analyst out there because I was not limited to any subset of securities. Scrolling through the OTCBB stock market lists of thousands of securities, I found a theme. I found US listed Chinese microcaps. When I looked at their financial statements it looked like companies that were growing at over 30% were trading at 2-3x earnings. I rejoiced. I thought that some of these companies could be 100-baggers. Due to my articles, investors had reached out to me looking for me to manage their money. A college friend's friend of mine gave me his limited partnership documents at a fee and I started a hedge fund. At it's peak, the AUM of the limited partnerships I managed was $10M.

"They can't all be fraud" I said to myself as I used my MBA and engineering skills to sort through them and of several hundred I was left with maybe a dozen or two dozen that I thought I could own. The rest I could identify simple accounting tricks that I had learned about by studying stories of accounting fraud. Overstating accounts receivable and the various ways to overstate income all stood out and so I was left with a handful of these US listed chinese companies that I thought were at least safe from accounting fraud. At the time I had not really understood that they would be able to get away with outright fraud. For the record, some of the companies financial statements matched my mentor's linear regression model with r^2 values of 0.99 (almost a perfect fit to a prediction model) which in retrospect should have indicated they were committing fraud but at the time I thought it just made them an incredibly predictable and reliable business.

I did a private placement in Longwei Petroleum and that would have worked out better if I was smarter about not trusting E*Trade's back office to convert my physical share certificates into tradable stock. At the time I didn't realize that the company was outright faking the financial statements and the auditors didn't seem to care enough to actually check anything. It was after this point that I started to get smarter about the quality of the auditors. This led me to China Media Express CCME.

China Media Express apparently was selling ads on busses and were doing really well. Deloitte was their auditor. Deloitte was one of the big 4 accounting firms and in theory their sign off on an audit actually meant something whereas the audits from the smaller audit firms in my view would only mean something if the big 4 audits could be trusted. It ended up that PricewaterhouseCoopers would do a forensic audit on China Media Express. My friend Zack Buckley had gone to China under Maj at GEO Investing and before he left he was bullish US listed Chinese microcaps and upon his return he didn't want to talk about them at all. He moved on and has succeeded elsewhere. This all culminated into one night at 3am I looked into the mirror after losing 20-30 lbs and only eating an egg or two a day and said, "Damnit Glen, you're not as smart as you think you are." I pressed the sell button on everything with the intention of shutting down my fund and returning money to my shareholders. I ended up getting my first stroke of luck. After dumping all of my CCME and half of my other US listed chinese companies (I was doing liquidity based selling with the goal of selling out entirely within a week or two) --- the morning I finished selling CCME it was halted pending the results of the forensic audit that basically reveled the company was faking income via recycling money through related party transactions at an increasing rate to fake increasing income.

It was at this point that I realized my theory of "they can't all be fraud" was probably false. I looked forward to moving back into my parent's house and crying while my mom held me. I figured that my skill of rapidly valuing companies would be in high demand. That was 2011. It's 2023 and I still have not really put that skill to use because the way the world works and the way I work although I do think that it will prove extremely valuable moving forward once the conservatorships are resolved.

Fraud To Understate Profits 2008-2011

The point of this section is to highlight my strong distaste to being defrauded. I have since determined at least my perspective is that the US listed chinese microcaps were faking their business statements to overstate their financials. I originally took a position in Fannie and Freddie because the reverse was true. John Hempton pointed out that Fannie and Freddie were overstating their losses at the hand of FHFA. I remember looking at this back in 2009 and thinking it was too complicated for me to figure out. I'm not a genius. I can't read financial statements well enough to be able to decipher what John Hempton was able to. What is interesting to me about John Hempton is that he was able to figure this out and even after figuring it out he only took a small position. The man is not only a genius in my view but also has wisdom beyond his years. I aspire to being able to read financial statements as well has he can. Only then can I begin to acquire the sort of wisdom that he has seemingly been able to accumulate.

The Conservatorships of Fannie Mae And Freddie Mac

My perspective in watching the conservatorships is that the law is an afterthought to government policy makers. This is evidenced by it being a novel idea when Mark Calabria marched around FHFA and encouraged everyone to follow the law when making decisions and determinations. Prior to him doing that it is unclear if considering the law was how any decisions got made. The priority of policy makers is to really just serve policy objectives.

Litigation History

The government has largely won the litigation brought by shareholders. Based on legal outcomes:

1. The government can take everything for nothing (APA Claims)
2. When it does --- it is not a takings in the court of federal claims
3. Shareholders cannot inspect the books and records of the companies
4. Shareholders cannot question the government's accounting 2008-2011.
    1. What is interesting about the accounting fraud lawsuits is the

government was furious that one of the auditors settled the suit brought by shareholders.

In my view, the takeaway of this litigation history is that conservatorship undermines established solvency law. FHFA can do whatever it wants. No one can ask questions. FHFA can run accounting schemes in the direct interest of Treasury. FHFA can give it all to Treasury for nothing.

The implication is that shareholders into the future can reasonably expect that when the companies exit from this conservatorship --- if they are ever placed into conservatorship again shareholders can look at history and discern the government can do whatever it wants and get away with it. In this context the Enterprise Regulatory Capital Framework (ERCF) that arguably overcapitalizes the enterprises given their risk/reward really serves as an economic incentive for shareholders to actually be willing to get involved here. For FDIC conservatorships that largely govern banks, one can expect that the conservator will not act in its own best interest at the expense of shareholders. That luxury is not afforded to investors in Fannie and Freddie. As such, upon exiting from conservatorship they can assume that their shares may only have future economic value as long as they can stay out of conservatorship. As such, overcapitalizing them with an obtuse capital framework in my view is the only way to attract investors in a world where the courts do not seem to even want to ultimately rule in favor of shareholder rights for these government sponsored enterprises. The courts, however, are not a complete loss for shareholders.

Trump Team: Started But Unfinished

When Trump was elected, his inbound Treasury Secretary Steven Mnuchin came out saying that one of the administration's priorities was to end the conservatorships of Fannie Mae and Freddie Mac. They did not succeed in ending the conservatorships under their watch, but they did set the companies on a path out of conservatorship via setting capital requirements and beginning the retention of earnings. Circumstances ultimately prevented Mnuchin from being willing to ultimately end the conservatorships on Calabria's watch and Trump's Treasury is not entirely blameless here. Mnuchin refused to work with prior FHFA director Watt, who would have been willing to begin the retention of earnings long before Trump could fire him. Mnuchin also refused to begin retaining earnings day one. As such, they got a late start of retaining earnings in September 2019.

Secondly, Mnuchin threw Calabria under the bus. Calabria wrote a book, Shelter From The Storm. Mnuchin could have settled the litigation, resolved the APA claims consistent with FDIC law and dismissed the interpretation of HERA that subsequently made the FHFA a political agency and got Calabria fired. That would have been a win for a historically accurate interpretation of the law. Instead, Trump's director of FHFA Mark Calabria, who was brought in to resolve the conservatorships after helping to write the law that governs them and papers on how the net worth sweep was illegal, was unable to complete the mission in its entirety. The Supreme Court ruling that makes FHFA a political agency is not a complete loss for shareholders though. Now the economic incentive for any particular presidential administration is to lock in their reforms by exiting conservatorship and to allocate the proceeds to further their own policy objectives.

CBO Report

I've probably read this August 2020 report dozens of times but most recently the part that I found the most interesting was that even though the report was published a year after the companies had begun retaining earnings and these additional retained earnings were reflected in the liquidation preference of the SPSPA, only the face value of the SPSPA was monetized in the theoretical recap and release scenarios. My view is that if the entire SPSPA liquidation preference is converted to common, commons have no intrinsic value, and so that is why I do not recommend them. That said, this CBO report, if taken literally, does seem to provide a path to there being some potential upside in common shares along with SPSPA face value being paid in full. Let's take a look into how that works in the context of the Housing Finance Blueprint. I'll run through the potential math and timeline of recap and release for Fannie Mae. Freddie Mac is running about 2 years behind Fannie Mae in terms of meeting preferred stock adjusted core capital requirements.

Fannie Mae: CBO Recap and Release Timeline Analysis

As of September 2019, Fannie Mae began retaining earnings in anticipation of eventually recapitalizing and release from conservatorship. Then they reported $10.3B of net worth. As of September 2023, Fannie Mae reported a net worth of $73.7B. Across 16 quarters Fannie Mae averaged $3.9B in earnings per quarter in that time period that grew their net worth. Fannie Mae has $19.1B of face value JPS and $120.8B of face value SPSPA. Their Tier 1 capital is -$59B but adjusted for preferred stock their capital is $80.9B and their Tier 1 capital requirements are $114B. As such, adjusting for preferred stock, Fannie Mae is $33.1B away from meeting their Tier 1 Capital requirements. As such, Fannie Mae can be forecasted to hit their Tier Tier 1 Capital requirements on an adjusted preferred stock basis in ~2 years or around the end of 2025.

At that time, their net worth would be around $108.8B. In my view, if the current presidential administration or the next presidential administration has not yet acted in its own best interest to lock in its policy objectives beyond conservatorship --- Treasury would begin actively defaulting on their agreement with Fannie Mae to allow them to raise third party capital and exit conservatorship. In my view, it is one thing to hold companies in conservatorship that do not have enough net worth to stand capitalized outside of it on their own. It is an entirely different thing, on the other hand, to actively sabotage the companies at the point where they can exit conservatorship without you by not following through on your good faith promise to them. As such, I think that it is around this time that we can expect Fannie Mae to exit conservatorship at the latest. So where does that put common share valuations at that point in time? Note that junior preferred would get face value based on the CBO report and currently trade around 10% of face value.

The CBO report envisions 6 separate scenarios with common-stock offerings in 2023 and 2025. This analysis was done well before we had a final ERCF capital rule. The beauty of this now is that we do not need to estimate the capital requirements. We can derive our own estimates using this model At a 10% investors' required return on capital on $15.8B of earnings the market cap of the common equity would be $158B. At an 8% required return on capital for investors the market cap of the equity would be $200B. The capital shortfall to full capital requirements of $71B at the end of 2025, but only $20B to meet Tier 1 capital requirements.

My understanding is Tier 1 capital requirements are the important ones and adjusted total capital really just regulates dividend paying power of the common equity securities. As the companies retain more money beyond core capital and Tier 1 capital requirements, they can pay out more of their total earnings, so to speak.

In the lower estimate at 10% cost of capital, $158B of market cap less $20B to Tier 1, $19B of JPS, $120.8B of SPSPA leaves nothing for existing common shares.

If cost of capital goes down and the market cap is $200B, I am calculating $41B of value would flow through to the warrants. $32B would belong to the US Treasury. Existing common shares would be worth around $6. In the theory that SPSPA can be paid down at face value and not liquidation preference, continued retained earnings seems to eventually accrue to the benefit of existing common shareholders once the government is able to get face value out of its SPSPA investment.

If you look at the government's own estimates of 2023 and 2025 equity offerings at 8% cost of capital and combined company earnings of Fannie and Freddie of $25B/annum they implicitly value common shares between $5 and $11 in their rosiest forecasts.

Takeaways from this CBO Analysis

There are a few takeaways from this analysis. The first of which would seem that if Mnuchin IPO'd Fannie and Freddie in 2021 like Calabria wanted, the government would not have gotten much financial incentive from doing so. The warrants in even the rosiest of rosy scenarios would have been worthless.

In fact, my understanding is that he would have had to take a hit on his SPSPA position in order to accomplish this and junior preferred shareholders were unwilling to take less than face which blocked the deal.

The second is that in any given administration, additional retained earnings throughout the administration as long as their is a recap and release at the end of the administration benefits that administration's policy objectives and maximizes their ability to spend and allocate the warrant money. Retained earnings on top of the SPSPA face value drive warrant proceeds which the government can allocate however it wants to achieve its objectives. In theory, the Biden administration would be better off recapping and releasing this coming year than any year prior.

Another takeaway is that this is a one time thing. The administration that executes the recap and release gets to spend the proceeds (if there are any). I think team Trump didn't have any. I think team Trump setup the Biden admin to be able to spend the warrant proceeds. I think team Trump could have unlocked these warrant proceeds for his administration a different way if Mnuchin would have settled the lawsuits --- but Mnuchin had political reasons for not taking the action necessary to achieve his beforementioned priorities.

Understanding Capital Structure

After winding up my hedge fund and becoming a normal employee again around 2011, I came across a Canadian Yellow Pages (phone book) company where the print business was in wind down and the digital business was replacing it. At the time I was a relative nobody but I tried to get shareholders to vote against a Chapter 11 style restructuring for the company. In retrospect I lucked out by not succeeding in my quest. I ended up owning preferred shares going into the restructuring and walked away with around $500k, i think a 5-10x return or somewhere in-between. It was this experience that taught me there is more than just P/E or PEG to a capital structure. EV/EBITDA is relevant to debtholders. For any given industry or business there is only so much DEBT/EBITDA that a company can hold. In a business that is in decline, sometimes 3.0x Debt/EBITDA is too much, but for a growth business they may be able to carry more than 5.0x.

I think there is a name for back to back Chapter 11's. At the time, two phone book companies in America filed back to back Chapter 11's as their financial forecasts deteriorated. I think their first series of restructurings refinanced their debt at 3.0x Debt/EBITDA and they still went under. More recently, due to the rise of interest rates this past year, I've watched a company that I owned go under with 5.0x Debt/EBITDA because the cost of interest gobbled up all their earnings on a forward basis.

The Relevant Equity Stack For Fannie and Freddie

As this relates to Fannie and Freddie and their restructuring, I previously owned junior preferred shares in a CBCA (Canadian equivalent to Chapter 11 in America). For Fannie and Freddie I own junior preferred shares in conservatorship, not to be confused with receivership. For Fannie and Freddie to evoke receivership would be to engage in a debt restructuring and this would be unsettling to capital markets. As such, the relevant parts of Fannie and Freddie's restructuring are:

1. Senior Preferred Stock (SPSPA) - Government Owned
2. Junior Preferred Stock - Shareholder Owned
3. Common Shares - Shareholder Owned
4. Warrants - Government Owned

The main feature of the Junior preferred shares that is attractive to me is their anti-dilution protection provisions, meaning that in order for Fannie and Freddie to raise capital, junior preferred have to be in the money.

In the CBO report, junior preferred get made whole even before the SPSPA gets made whole.

Administrative Reform

Prior CFO Timothy J Howard talks about the Biden admin moving forward with recap and release:

Will they embrace that way out? I wish I knew. But "kicking the can down the road" won't result in a better resolution than the one I've proposed, and it WILL result in some other administration getting the credit (and the value of Treasury's warrants for 79.9 percent of the companies' common stock) for whatever that resolution ultimately turns out to be.

Prior Obama Official David H Stevens is more direct about protecting the companies from the direction of a non-democratic FHFA director:

I think the growing call to release the GSE's warrants attention by the administration. Clearly there is increased concern about the risks of an endless array of politically motivated FHFA Directors tinkering with these important companies. Release is the only option to protect them.

So, no future administration can change the overall resolution of conservatorship and the Biden administration only stands to gain by ending the conservatorships. If Biden doesn't take action this term, I would argue that the next presidential term forces the end of the conservatorships.

My Personal Position

When I first took a position in Fannie and Freddie I bought common shares on the back of seeing Bill Ackman's 2014 111 page slide deck. Originally, I invested based on the idea that the applicable law and their continued forward earnings would only further undermine the government's deception surrounding the net worth sweep. Little did I know at the time that it didn't even matter --- because the government can do whatever it wants.

The last time I think I disclosed my personal position was April 18, 2021 in anticipation of the Supreme Court Summer 2021 being a huge victory for shareholders. I was wrong.

The Supreme Court decided that FHFA can do whatever it wants which at the very least undermines insolvency law for Fannie and Freddie. That is to say that if Fannie and Freddie are ever placed into conservatorship again, you can expect to kiss your butt goodbye if you're a shareholder. Leading up to the Supreme Court ruling I was confident that shareholder interests would prevail, but if worse came to worse I could always prioritize my payment schedule.

My Financial Position In Summer of 2021

At that point I stated that I owned 7,400 OTCQB:FMCCG, 550 OTCQB:FMCCH, 4,508 OTCQB:FMCCI, 1,375 OTCQB:FMCCL, 2,105 OTCQB:FMCCM, 398 OTCQB:FMCCN, 3,259 OTCQB:FMCCP, 5,280 OTCQB:FMCCS, 3,300 OTCQB:FMCKP, 3,916 FNMAO, 41,333 OTCQB:FNMAP and 5 OTCPK:FNMFO. This was $4.1M of par value of preferred stock. Given that for the most part I had rolled into Fannie and Freddie in 2014 with $500K and been buying ever since and even borrowed somewhere around $150-250k to buy as much as I could when FNMAS dipped to $5 using income based personal loans and credit cards. So, not only was I carrying this debt, but I also had banked roughly $50k in a roth 401k after working roughly 8 years at a full time job. Needless to say, all of my earnings were going to debt service and I was basically treading water without having to sell stock heading into the Supreme Court ruling, maximum position and maximum confidence.

Sort of 'Quitting My Job'

The Supreme Court ruling came out and undermined solvency law. The price collapsed. The preferreds that were at 25% of face value went to 5% of face value. Instead of 4x upside to par there was 20x upside to par. At these prices, if I quit my job and rolled my 401k to a self directed Roth IRA I could buy $1,000,000 in par. In other words, I believed I would eventually make a million dollars to quit my job that I had worked 8 years or so for and not had made a million dollars working my job in that time. Cool beans. I ended up quitting my full-time position and switching to a contract only basis so I could make that trade. W-2 to W-9.

Temporarily Strategically Defaulted On Debt

After making that trade, I thought to myself "this is easy --- what else can I do?" I stopped making payments on my debt. I went into default. The same companies that comprised FM Watch that were part of running Fannie and Freddie into the ground were some of my creditors. My thought process is that if the government can play dirty, I can too. In my view, the legislative branch in 2008 passed a decently fair law, HERA, that created FHFA from

OFHEO. The problem is that in 2012 the White House enacted the net worth sweep and in 2014 and 2021 the judicial branch didn't stand up for the law either. As such, what they did in my view was not honoring the spirit of the law or the contracts and the big banks were the ones pulling the strings. I defaulted on my debt for around a year or so and have since started making payments again to pay it down, but in that year I probably accumulated another million or so in par value by just temporarily defaulting and destroying my credit. My view was --- is getting another million dollars more important than having an 800 credit score? I decided that was a yes.

Multiple Contract Jobs

Staring down the barrel of a 20x return will make you go nuts. At least it did for me. In my view, every month I worked and banked that money into Fannie and Freddie jps was equivalent to just working 20 months and saving it in a savings account. If prices stayed that low for a year I could bank 20 years in a single year!

I immediately started working 16 hours per day doing two full time jobs on a contract basis. Now I was banking like 40 years in a single year, an entire lifetime of work in a single year compared to where I was the year before. This was exhausting, but I was making more money than ever before and contract work pays more and on an accelerated schedule. This supercharged my purchases of Fannie and Freddie during a time when they were trading at a 15-20x discount to par.

Life Catches Up

Another driver of incremental par value is my Grandmother died and left me money. Another million of par value there. She was an incredible woman who grew up an orphan and built a strong family and always set a strong example of how to be a good person and I have so many fond memories of her and would prefer to have her around than the par value but that choice is not available to me. From 2014-2021 I had put my life on hold, played by the rules and generally had hoped that I would get things together so that my grandmother could meet my firstborn child. Unfortunately things took to long and she was never able to. I became a father earlier this year.

I never really expected things to get so backwards that I would have to prioritize payments this way or play so aggressive. That said, I am just following incentives and taking notes on how the world works and playing the way I see the world work around me and so far so good.

My Incremental Views On Position Sizing

Since 2014 I generally have had over 100% of my net worth in Fannie and Freddie preferred. There have been times when I was under 100% or was swing trading other securities, but it was always with the sole purpose of just being able to acquire more Fannie and Freddie preferred.

Generally speaking if I had not taken a 100% position in Fannie and Freddie I would have been able to buy dips, given the volatility of these securities and the duration that this trade has taken (9 years and counting), I would be more than twice better off. I was looking back through and because I leveraged up with debt I spent like 3-4 years treading water unable to increase my position size because I tried to lever up and buy more on leverage in prior years.

This ate up all of my walk around money so to speak. In fact, I even put off dental work and walked right into two teeth falling out and three root canals. Putting your life on hold on a 'temporary' basis that extends itself 9 years leads to a very suboptimal life and disjointed day-to-day life decision making.

My View On Pair Trading

My biggest loss of opportunity cost is probably not taking a more sizable position in the liquid jps FNMAS and FMCKJ and pair scale trading them using the prebuilt interactive brokers automatic pairs scale trader. I could have probably generated $10K+/annum setting that up if not more if I would have dedicated my entire portfolio to it. Life probably would have been more fun throughout this trade as well.

How This Worked Out For Me

Really only the last two years mattered. The prior 7 were wasted. Wasting 7 years is a lot of time. I was too far from family. I made low six figures but lived on cheap groceries and didn't date despite being in the prime of my life and having the financial capacity to. That's not financially wise, but it ended up working out. I'm a dad now. I've got more par than ever. From here, life is not too bad.

Current Share Allocations

I now have 6581 FMCCG, 6135 FMCCI, 89596 FMCCJ, 1672 FMCCK, 35918 FMCCM, 14406 FMCCN, 2401 FMCCO, 111223 FMCCS, 28905 FMCKJ, 50 FNMAO, 825 FNMAP, 5 FNMFO, 773 FREGP and 100 FREJN or $14.7M in par value. I've been able to take down $10M in additional par value because the Supreme Court in my opinion misinterpreted the law. Maybe instead of complaining about them I should thank them. Thanks guys and gals. That said, I'm still not making money in this trade despite putting everything I have into this since 2014. I think my financial breakeven from a technical perspective for people who care about that sort of thing (I don't think it's valuable information, but Billy Walters might.) occurs around $FNMAS hitting $4.

Summary and Conclusion

My 9 year trade in Fannie and Freddie has grown long in the tooth but I have dug in my heels and made the most of it and I believe the best is yet to come and the market is a fool for pricing junior preferred the way it has the past two years. Fine by me. I know a bargain when I see one.

I grew up in the Midwest and was naive and just assumed that there was a system of checks and balances that ultimately followed the law here in America and so this has been a learning experience not only about how the world works but also how hard I am willing to work to see a successful outcome, which has not yet arrived but I believe is en route.

We are now firmly in the hands of admin reform either this administration or the next. Either way, junior preferred get made whole. If Biden follows incentives, that will be this next year. 10x. Can't go wrong with that. It's one thing to keep a company in conservatorship because it does not meet capital requirements. It is entirely something else to keep a company in conservatorship once it does - or worse, to force them to stay in conservatorship once they have met the capital requirements to exit. Based on my analysis, the current pricing of the preferred does not accurately reflect the time that it takes to get there.

Inflation, Housing Crisis, And GSE Conservatorship: A Path Forward

Summary
- Rising home prices, inflation concerns, and housing shortages highlight the urgency for GSE reform, aligning with proposed solutions from Democratic housing experts.
- White House signals, including statements from key officials like Brian Deese and Lael Brainard, indicate a growing focus on housing policy, potentially paving the way for GSE recapitalization and release.
- Fannie Mae and Freddie Mac remain in conservatorship since 2008, with recent efforts focused on their responsible exit. Legal battles and political shifts suggest a potential path toward release.

Bloomberg/Bloomberg via Getty Images

Fannie Mae (OTCQB:FNMA) and Freddie Mac (OTCQB:FMCC) are two companies in conservatorship retaining their earnings since September 2019 on their path out of conservatorship. Combined they now have over $125B in net worth which is an all-time record high. Since the companies have begun retaining earnings, the FHFA has been diligently preparing them to responsibly exit conservatorship. Over the years, numerous lawsuits have challenged the government's actions during conservatorship. In August of last year, a jury decided that the government acted in bad faith when arranging the net worth sweep. Since then, prior Democratic White House housing officials have come out separately saying that the conservatorship should end as well as how they would allocate $90B to solve the nation's affordable housing crisis. In fact, the CEO of Fannie Mae came out associating ending the conservatorship with a victory lap.

Investment Thesis

The litigation so far and the pending litigation has not and probably will not result in the legal system forcing the government to release Fannie Mae and Freddie Mac from conservatorship. The Trump administration came up 6 months to a year too short from being able to restructure and effectuate an equity offering. While I believe that it is true that if Trump becomes president again, releasing Fannie and Freddie from conservatorship is a sure thing, I think that the politics are concurrently heating up to drive Biden admin action. Further, I believe the steps the Biden administration has taken to prepare the companies to exit conservatorship points to where things are headed despite the administration not explicitly prioritizing resolving the conservatorships.

For the Biden administration to move forward with recapitalizing and releasing Fannie and Freddie from conservatorship, housing needs to gain steam as a political issue. With there being a housing supply shortage and inflation running high, this sets the stage for a victory lap where the government's equity stake is restructured and the proceeds go to increasing housing supply and thus combating inflation. In any restructuring via recap and release where the government is able to monetize its equity position, junior preferred would be made whole and common would potentially have upside if the government decides to write down their SPSPA liquidation preference or if the equity markets value reformed GSEs with higher than historical valuations. Junior preferred shares currently trade at ~15% of face value.

Fannie Mae FY 2023 Earnings Highlights

The CEO of Fannie Mae Priscilla Almodovar pointed out that the companies have been profitable on a quarterly basis for 24 quarters in a row:

The fourth quarter capped another successful year. Fannie Mae reported $3.9 billion in net income, marking our twenty-fourth consecutive quarter of positive earnings

Since they have been able to retain all their earnings, their net worth has exploded higher since 2019, not bad for a company in conservatorship:

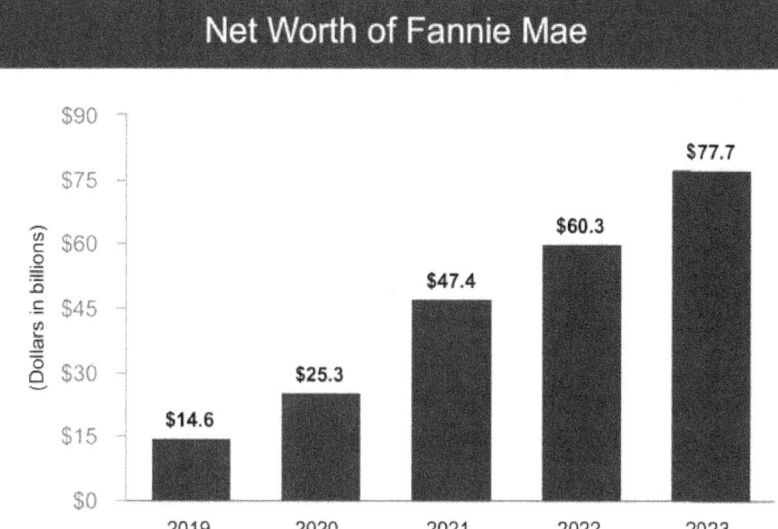

Fannie Mae Net Worth (Fannie Mae Net Worth)

Fannie Mae has been retaining tens of billions of dollars a year. The earnings press release also points out increasing home prices:
- Home prices grew 7.1% on a national basis in 2023 according to the Fannie Mae Home Price Index

This factors into higher inflation and affordability as the CEO pointed out:

It was a challenging year for housing, with higher mortgage rates, limited homes for sale, and high home prices weighing on affordability.

Should the Biden administration take action to increase housing supply and decrease mortgage rates through administrative recap and release, more Americans could find their way into home ownership.

Freddie Mac FY 2023 Earnings Highlights

The third bullet point in Freddie Mac's 2023 earnings report summary indicates the continued benefit to Freddie Mac's earnings of rising home prices.
- Net income of $2.9 billion, an increase of 65% year-over-year, primarily driven by higher net revenues and a credit reserve release in Single-Family in the fourth quarter of 2023 compared to a credit reserve build in Single-Family in the fourth quarter of 2022.

- Net revenues of $5.4 billion, an increase of 11% year-over-year, driven by higher net interest income and non-interest income.
- Benefit for credit losses of $0.5 billion, primarily driven by a credit reserve release in Single-Family due to improvements in house prices.

While Freddie Mac and Fannie Mae benefit from rising home prices, home prices are a large factor driving inflation. Thus, it would be a political victory to allocate money to increasing housing supply and all the more reason to believe the Biden admin would at least want to take action. Freddie Mac now has a net worth of $47.7B and has been profitable for many years and should no longer be held in conservatorship.

Fannie Mae CEO: Exiting Conservatorship = A Victory Lap

The CEO of Fannie Mae on January 19 equated the end of conservatorship with a Victory Lap.

Fannie Mae CEO Victory Lap (Fannie Mae CEO Victory Lap)

Prior FHFA director James Lockhart had previously told Inside Mortgage Finance that this was precisely the sort of public commentary the CEOs should be engaging in:

This was precisely the sort of public commentary that former Federal Housing Finance Agency Director James Lockhart recently told Inside Mortgage Finance the GSEs should be engaging in. He said that, despite the edict against lobbying by the GSEs, as long as they don't ask for specific votes, it's fine for them to educate Congress and the public about issues like the conservatorship.

Prior Democrat Admin Officials

James Parrott and David H Stevens are two prior Democratic leaders of housing finance reform issues.

James Parrott

James Parrott served as a senior advisor at the National Economic Council (NEC) in the Obama White House. He led the team of advisers charged with counseling the cabinet and president on housing issues during one of the most tumultuous times in the history of housing policy, helping them navigate through the collapse of the housing market and the early days of GSE reform. On February 12, he has written with Mark Zandi on how to solve the nation's affordable housing crisis. He estimates that his plan would put millions of families into homes:

Taken together, these moves would trigger a dramatic increase in the supply and affordability of entry-level homes and put millions of families into position to take advantage of it.

He estimates the ultimate cost to be $90B:

This would be an aggressive effort, costing as much as roughly $90 billion over the next decade, according to our budget analysis, depending on how aggressive Congress wants to be.

Note that this $90B cost would seem to be covered by the CBO's estimate of what the government's warrants would be worth $100B. As such, it would seem there is a potential solution here being advocated by influential Democratic housing experts that costs about the same amount that the government would reap from ending the conservatorships.

David H Stevens

David H Stevens was the former assistant secretary of Housing and FHA commissioner under President Obama. In December, he wrote in favor of ending the conservatorships:

HERA explicitly provided guidelines for FHFA to take the GSEs out of conservatorship.

...

But ultimately FHFA has the authority - even a duty - under HERA to take the GSEs out of conservatorship, working with the Treasury which holds its preferred stock.

...

FHFA and the Treasury should release the GSEs from conservatorship as soon as possible.

David H Stevens has been advocating for the end of the conservatorships since the Supreme Court ruled that FHFA is a political agency in June 2021. My last correspondence with him before he passed last month was a message from him, "Well done" with reference to my most recent article that he contributed to. I wish we still had his voice to push this forward. Regardless of personal opinions on his message, he held a unique ability to captivate listeners. Reluctantly, I must acknowledge his prophetic accuracy, making his absence felt even more deeply.

Janet Yellen Hearing Testimony

On February 6, Treasury's Janet Yellen attended a House Financial Services committee where she answered some questions on Fannie and Freddie:

Mr. FitzGerald: When Fannie Mae and Freddie Mac were taken into conservatorship in 2008, Treasury received warrants that give it the right to buy common stock in each of the GSEs equal to 80% of the total outstanding shares and those warrants expire in September 7 of 2028. In August of 2020 the Congressional Budget Office issued a report that estimated Treasury could receive the $190B for its Senior Preferred shares in addition to $110 billion from exercising its warrants in the GSEs. FHFA Director Thompson in the hearing last May said that the two of you have not discussed these warrants. The conservatorship has gone on for -- I think you could agree -- probably too long now. I am concerned that the conservatorship of the GSEs and the warrants could be used to further politicize the entities. Have you or your staff given any consideration to the monetization of Treasury's warrants in the GSEs?

Janet Yellen: This is not a matter that I'm up to speed on. I'm not knowledgeable about this. I have a staff that spends a great deal of time thinking about it but I've not had a discussion with them about this. I would appreciate it if I could get back to you on this matter.

What we can see from this is that there are staff at Treasury who spend a great deal of time thinking about what to do with Treasury's equity stake in Fannie and Freddie. Also, it is my view that Treasury is not in the driver's seat of administrative reform. Direction would come from the White House. Who is to say why Janet Yellen's staff has been spending all this time looking at the valuation of Treasury's equity position. It is hard to imagine it being relevant unless there is interest from the White House.

White House National Economic Council Observations

In my view, there have been indications from within the White House that support the path of the Biden administration moving recap and release.

Prior Biden WH NEC Director Brian Deese

Brian Deese posted on twitter late last year that we need to take action on housing now.

We need more active fiscal policy on housing. We need to incentivize the building of affordable housing. We should do that now, and not admire the problem in 2025/26/27.

To provide context around the gravitas of Brian Deese and James Parrott, they both originally worked on the third amendment net worth sweep.

Bowler testified that prior to finalizing the Third Amendment, "as Treasury Staff negotiated with FHFA staff, the Treasury staff . . . would propose the National Economic Council as to developments and the two people that we proposed would be Brian Deese and Jim Parrott.

It would appear that the two leading White House officials who orchestrated the net worth sweep to keep the companies in conservatorship may be setting the stage for their exit.

WH NEC Director Lael Brainard

Lael Brainard for the first time in the Biden administration publicly addressed housing in December of last year. That's notable in its own right. She spoke about fully utilizing their administrative authorities to address the challenge of housing affordability:

Our first major priority is increasing the supply of affordably priced homes in order to lower housing costs. We are using every lever at our disposal - legislative proposals, **our administrative authorities**, our convening power, and our bully pulpit - to do so.

But **we cannot wait for Congress to act**. Through our Housing Supply Action Plan, we are reducing barriers to housing and offering new and improved financing for affordable housing development.

In August, Daniel Hornung was promoted within the NEC as the housing guy. Further, the White House CEA director Jared Bernstein previously wrote about how to structure recap and release:

The key, then, is to a) put private capital in a "first loss" position ahead of the government, and b) set a price for the government insurance that accurately reflects and offsets the expected taxpayer costs of the backstop, something the GSEs decidedly did not do.

The White House definitely has definitely been spending more time on housing the past year. This past week Lael Brainard came out saying that they are still struggling to convince the American public that they are winning the battle against inflation and that

Americans are "fed up" with high prices for everyday purchases such as many food products and housing, and said the Biden administration would seek to push them down

The administration has the political lever through its controlling interest in Fannie and Freddie to increase housing supply and task Fannie and Freddie to buy down mortgage rates to fight inflation and increase affordability.

Recent Legal Developments

Bhatti v. FHFA had oral arguments February 14 before the Eighth Circuit that you can listen to here. If you are interested in the summary of what is going on there --- they are basically disputing the Collins ruling. There is a letter that summarizes their argument below:

Cooper & Kirk
Lawyers
A Professional Limited Liability Company

1523 New Hampshire Avenue, N.W.
Washington, D.C. 20036

(202) 220-9600
Fax (202) 220-9601

February 12, 2024

VIA CM/ECF

Michael E. Gans
Clerk of Court
U.S. Court of Appeals for the Eighth Circuit
111 South 10th Street, Room 24.329
St. Louis, MO 63102

Re: *Bhatti et al. v. Federal Housing Finance Agency et al.*, No. 23-1051
Rule 28(j) Notice of Supplemental Authority (Oral Argument Set for February 14, 2024, in St. Paul before Judges Smith, Benton, and Stras)

Dear Mr. Gans:

Plaintiffs-Appellants respectfully respond to Defendants-Appellees' notice of supplemental authority regarding *Collins v. Dep't of Treasury*, 83 F.4th 970 (5th Cir. 2023).

The Fifth Circuit's ultimate disposition in *Collins* was at odds with its reasoning, which in fact supports Plaintiffs' entitlement to relief. The Fifth Circuit held that "the complaint plausibly alleges," *id.* at 984, that "after two years with Calabria as the head of the FHFA—the Trump Administration would have held a public offering of shares, and that offering would likely have resulted in the elimination of the Treasury's liquidation preferences," *id.*; *see also id.* at 983 ("[T]he amended complaint alleges that the Trump Administration would have eliminated the liquidation preferences in preparation for a public offering of shares that was scheduled to take place in 2021, roughly two years after Director Calabria took office."). This reasoning cannot be squared with the Fifth Circuit's ultimate disposition. What the Fifth Circuit found shareholders to have plausibly alleged is precisely what Plaintiffs must show to survive a motion to dismiss.

Respectfully submitted,

/s/ Brian W. Barnes
Brian W. Barnes

Counsel for Plaintiffs-Appellants

Cc: All Counsel of Record

Eighth Circuit Court Letter (Eighth Circuit Court Letter)

So far the legal system has not been impressed with this line of reasoning in the fifth circuit. It will be interesting to see if the Eighth circuit court agrees with plaintiffs.

Timing & Catalysts

Tim Pagliara, an activist shareholder, is optimistic the Biden administration will start politicizing housing affordability and inflation and that this will bring GSE recap and release to the table as an actionable solution and that the State of the Union address by Biden will be revealing:

Bloomberg reports the recapitalization and release of the GSE's as a "Trump" trade. I believe it is the Biden trade. March 7, SOTU is one of the latest ever scheduled. Watch Housing and the shortage of single family homes become a major theme. Biden will call for a recommitment to the American Dream of home ownership. Recap, release, monetization of the warrants will be part of the solution.

Two days before the SOTU address, Super Tuesday will likely determine Trump officially wins the Republican party's nomination. Fannie and Freddie junior preferred shares still trade at a significant discount to his election probabilities. In theory this gap should close or there until there is less money to be arbitraged out of Shorting Trump election odds and going long Fannie and Freddie junior preferred. For those skeptical that Trump would move forward with recap and release he did write a letter saying he would have but he ran out of time:

DONALD J. TRUMP

November 11, 2021

The Honorable Rand Paul
United States Senate
Washington, D.C.

Dear Senator Paul,

Thank you for talking to me about the need to privatize Fannie Mae and Freddie Mac, two great American companies, and about the question the Supreme Court has raised about what I would have been able to accomplish if I had been able to fire the incompetent Mel Watt from day one of my Administration.

Another Obama/Biden scam in legal trouble was when they allowed the Federal Housing Finance Agency (FHFA) to steal the retirement savings of hardworking Americans who had invested in Fannie Mae and Freddie Mac. In a recent ruling, the Supreme Court has recognized that my Administration was denied the ability to oversee the work of FHFA in violation of the Constitution. The Supreme Court's decision asks what I would have done had I controlled FHFA from the beginning of my Administration, as the Constitution required. From the start, I would have fired former Democrat Congressman and political hack Mel Watt from his position as Director and would have ordered FHFA to release these companies from conservatorship. My Administration would have also sold the government's common stock in these companies at a huge profit and fully privatized the companies. The idea that the government can steal money from its citizens is socialism and is a travesty brought to you by the Obama/Biden administration. My Administration was denied the time it needed to fix this problem because of the unconstitutional restriction on firing Mel Watt. It has to come to an end and courts must protect our citizens.

Sincerely,

Trump Letter (Trump Letter)

In another Trump administration, with 5+ years of retained earnings and FHFA as a political appointee, recap and release in my view is a sure thing. This doesn't even take into account that Fannie Mae is expected to hit statutory minimum capital on a preferred stock adjusted basis in the next year and a half. How do you keep a company like that in conservatorship?

Treasury FY 2023 Budget

The government published its updated FY 2023 valuation of its senior preferred stock in both companies on February 15:

Note 8. Investments in Government-Sponsored Enterprises

Investments in GSEs as of September 30, 2023

(In billions of dollars)	Gross Investments	Cumulative Valuation Gain/(Loss)	Fair Value
Fannie Mae senior preferred stock	190.4	(55.9)	134.5
Freddie Mac senior preferred stock	114.4	(12.7)	101.7
Fannie Mae warrants common stock	3.1	(0.4)	2.7
Freddie Mac warrants common stock	2.3	(0.8)	1.5
Total investments in GSEs	310.2	(69.8)	240.4

Investments in GSEs as of September 30, 2022

(In billions of dollars)	Gross Investments	Cumulative Valuation Gain/(Loss)	Fair Value
Fannie Mae senior preferred stock	177.7	(62.0)	115.7
Freddie Mac senior preferred stock	106.6	(2.1)	104.5
Fannie Mae warrants common stock	3.1	(0.9)	2.2
Freddie Mac warrants common stock	2.3	(1.0)	1.3
Total investments in GSEs	289.7	(66.0)	223.7

Treasury FY 2023 Balance Sheet Note 8 (Treasury FY 2023 Balance Sheet Note 8)

The government increased the FV of its senior preferred stock due to higher projected cash flows:

The FV of the senior preferred stock-as measured by unobservable and observable inputs-increased as of September 30, 2023, when compared to September 30, 2022. Fannie Mae's senior preferred stock drove this increase primarily due to higher projected cash flows and a decrease in credit-related expenses.

The Treasury report continues:

To date, Congress has not passed legislation nor has FHFA taken action to end the GSEs' conservatorships.

It looks like Treasury is blaming FHFA as the party responsible for needing to take action while FHFA is saying it needs someone at Treasury to help restructure the SPSPA agreement. Seeing as how both federal agencies are controlled by the White House, this seems more like a pending policy decision while both federal agencies wait for the green light.

Summary & Conclusion

Administrative action with respect to Fannie Mae and Freddie Mac has been a long time coming ever since Mark Calabria worked with Steven Mnuchin to begin the retention of earnings in 2019. Inflation is a real problem with rising home prices and this also exacerbates the affordable housing crisis:

One of the most important issues in the President's economic agenda - lowering costs and increasing access to housing for Americans.

...

Our first major priority is increasing the supply of affordably priced homes in order to lower housing costs.

It would seem to me that they should want to monetize their equity position to solve the funding problem. Treasury staff seem to be actively engaged in valuing Treasury's equity position. The companies may have $125B of net worth (All-time record high), but the government still has not officially let them go and raise capital and exit conservatorship. When they do, shareholders stand to benefit and the CBO report suggests junior preferred specifically can expect face value. The only step left to really kickstarting administrative action is raising awareness. Here's to helping make affordable housing and fighting inflation more visible political priorities so that the government can take the victory lap.

Future Of Fannie Mae And Freddie Mac Post-2024 Election

Summary

- Fannie Mae and Freddie Mac have been trapped in conservatorship since 2008, with the government aggressively manipulating asset values to justify seizing control early in conservatorship.
- The Trump administration began recapitalization efforts, and under Biden, earnings have continued to accumulate, positioning the GSEs for a potential exit from conservatorship.
- Moelis' 2024 update suggests a new administration could quickly restructure Fannie and Freddie, with junior preferred shareholders likely to be made whole.
- The legal system has largely abandoned GSE shareholders' rights but retained earnings and potential equity restructuring offer hope for junior preferred shareholders.

mphillips007/iStock via Getty Images

Fannie Mae (OTCQB:FNMA) and Freddie Mac (OTCQB:FMCC) are two government-sponsored enterprises (GSEs) that have been in conservatorship since September 6, 2008. Hank Paulson and Dan Jester led Treasury's efforts to seize the companies and restructure their balance sheets to inject capital via the SPSPA, an agreement that was put in place after they were put in conservatorship that relied on FHFA's discretionary accounting authority to write down GSE assets to support the narrative of the enterprises needing capital.

The government, for its support, gave itself the SPSPA and 79.9% warrants at a nominal strike price. The next 3 years, the government systematically wrote down the value of the GSE assets, pretending that they were going out of business. In 2012, the government ran out of discretionary writedowns and also ran out of time to shutter Fannie and Freddie as the housing market was rebounding, and it arranged with itself to take all of the profits of Fannie and Freddie for nothing via the net worth sweep. The Supreme Court in 2021 ruled that the net worth sweep was legal. The Court of Federal Claims declared that the net worth sweep was not a taking, either. The only legal claims that are currently prevailing are the breach of implied covenant of good faith, which apparently forgot to include reliance damages in their damage model and so the damages awarded to the shareholder plaintiffs are a few quarters on a $25 preferred, which is like a missing dividend payment, sort of joke if you will for a violated contract. So, why bother owning anything at all here?

Investment Thesis

In September 2019, the government under Trump triggered the beginning of the process of recap and release by retaining earnings. Under Biden, earnings have continued to pile up on the enterprise's balance sheets. Earlier this year, Fannie Mae CEO said, "(s)omeone somewhere has not taken a victory lap for the work that has been done to rehabilitate the enterprises" while contemplating a future outside of conservatorship. Meanwhile, the Biden administration has prioritized addressing housing as a political issue but has largely so far overlooked that it could fund it if it chose to monetize its position in Fannie and Freddie and allocate the warrant proceeds to incentivize the build out of affordable housing supply nationwide despite this plan being detailed to FHFA's Sandra Thompson. In any equity restructuring where the conservatorship ends outside of receivership, junior preferred shareholders would be made whole. Common shareholder returns are subject to dilution, potentially significant enough such that I think they largely lack security and am personally not recommending them and I don't own any myself, but wish good luck to those who do.

Illustrative Capital Raise Timeline

Moelis put out an update a few months ago in May 2024 outlining how quickly Fannie and Freddie could be restructured by the incoming administration, leading to offerings early 2026:

Illustrative Capital Raise Timeline

Fannie Mae
Freddie Mac

Given the quantum of retained earnings, and the years of advance planning put-in during Trump's first term, a 1 year timeline is possible. Key considerations include: 1) Conversion terms, 2) Ongoing MBS market support

	2025				2026		2027		$Capital	%Asset[2]
	Q1	Q2	Q3	Q4	H1	H2	H1	H2		
Announce future, not immediate, exit from conservatorship	◆									
Write-off SPS balance (to reflect original contractual terms) or equitize SPS		◆							$185bn	2.2%
Agree to terms to of JPS treatment (e.g., equitization), and PSPA commitment		◆	◆							
Establish regulatory framework and mechanics for oversight of G-fees		◆	◆							
Companies issue primary common equity through an IPO					◆				$35bn	0.4%
Companies issue new junior preferred stock					◆				$35bn	0.4%
GSEs emerge as rebuilt organizations and taxpayers profitably exit their only remaining financial crisis federal financial assistance					◆				$255bn	3.0%
Treasury sells remaining equity interest via secondary offerings						◆	◆	◆	~$150bn proceeds	

Selected Additional Considerations:
- Away from value attribution, selected key considerations include:
  - Status of PSPA Commitment (and related commitment fees, as applicable)
  - Logistics associated with JPS conversion (e.g. 2/3 thresholds for amendments carrots and/or sticks to incent participation
  - Guidance on guarantee fees (including raises to offset any PSPA commitment fees, and/or to improve profitability, as well as any regulatory limitations
  - Imposition of any consent decree or other limitations on the post-conservatorship GSEs

Moelis

Illustrative Capital Raise Timeline (GSE Discussion Material - May 2024 - Moelis)

Moelis points out in their plan:

- During the duration of President Biden's first term in office, the FHFA has made substantial progress in positioning the GSEs for a scenario in which they are no longer under conservatorship
- These efforts included finalizing regulatory capital rules, effectively navigating the post-COVID recovery, and achieving $125bn of combined book value through retained earnings
- However, despite these positive movements, the Biden Administration has shown little-to-no desire to exit the GSEs from conservatorship to date
- As we approach election season, we want to revisit where the GSEs currently stand today and an illustrative framework for a post-election recapitalization and exit from conservatorship

Key Observations

There were a few key observations from the recent Moelis update.

Firstly, a new administration would no longer be burdened by having to do the heavy lifting that the Trump administration had to start with:

- Any settlement and transaction could now occur at the front-end of a new administration, not the tail end

For those unfamiliar, Trump was unable to complete the recap and release of Fannie and Freddie in his first term. For starters, Collins v. Yellen had not yet been ruled on by the Supreme Court, so he was not able to fire Mel Watt on day one. Secondly, they would have been able to get it done but COVID-19 allegedly, according to Craig Phillips and Mark Calabria, delayed it too much, and it ended up being left undone. The companies now have retained 5 years of capital and a lot of the work has been done to prepare them to exit conservatorship, so it is really turnkey at this point.

Secondly, BTIG's Isaac Boltansky points out that given the capital build, an incoming Democrat administration could also be supportive of recap and release:

We continue to firmly believe that a Republican White House will prioritize ending the GSE conservatorship given the commentary during the Trump administration. We have viewed a second term for President Biden as far less constructive for GSE shareholders given his Treasury Department's disinterest to date, but we are now increasingly optimistic that administrative GSE reform could fit neatly on a Biden II policy agenda as well.

It remains unclear if a democrat administration would support recap and release from conservatorship.

Trump Surely Supports Recap and Release

On March 27, 2019, Trump issued a Memorandum on Federal Housing Finance Reform where the first section reads:

Section 1. Framework to Reform the GSEs. (A) The Secretary of the Treasury is hereby directed to develop a plan for administrative and legislative reforms (Treasury Housing Reform Plan) to achieve the following housing reform goals:

(i) Ending the conservatorships of the GSEs upon the completion of specified reforms;

On November 11, 2021, Trump wrote a letter to senator Rand Paul:

The Supreme Court's decision asks what I would have done had I controlled FHFA from the beginning of my Administration, as the Constitution required. From the start I would have fired former Democrat Congressman and political hack Mel Watt from his position as Director and would have ordered FHFA to release these companies from conservatorship. My administration would have also sold the government's common stock in these companies at a huge profit and fully privatized the companies.

Republicans Looking For Recap and Release Plan

Most recently, Republican Warren Davidson has been asking Janet Yellen about the report due to Congress at the Financial Stability Oversight Council Hearing, two years and counting. This most recent time, he pointed out that the report was due September 30, 2021. He asked Janet Yellen if Treasury could commit to giving Congress the plan. Her response was that it was a promise made by the previous administration. His response was that it was a statutory requirement.

Whatever the plan is, it is already the law to give us the plan.

So far, under Biden, Treasury has still not submitted the plan to Congress. As such, the most recent plan was put together in September 2019, largely by Craig Phillips. As far as I can tell, nothing about the restructuring and recap and release path has materially changed since then.

Election Probabilities

If you assume that an incoming Democrat administration would not end the conservatorships and would be followed by similarly Democratic administrations into the future, the only path to resolution of the conservatorships would be an incoming Trump administration. If you assume that the junior preferred would be made whole two years from today as part of the equity offering and a 10% discount rate. The value of $FNMAS, which has a $25 par value, if we were 100% confident that Trump would win the election, would be $20. $FNMAS currently trades at $4.25. This seems to suggest that junior preferreds are predicting that Trump has less than 25% chance of winning the incoming election. Most of the polls all seem to agree that election odds are closer to 50/50 which would put $FNMAS closer to $10.

I'm not a polling expert, but I have started following Rasmussen Reports, who puts out their polling data on a daily basis and has been explaining what they do to their polling data to take out any bias that they can observably detect and frankly their analysis at face value sounds pretty reasonable. They are currently arguing that Trump's election odds are over 50%. They also have been vocal in regard to their criticisms of the polling industry and how aggregators, based on their analysis, are biased. That said, the most optimistic poll I was able to find for Harris was she was leading Trump by 7 points. Even if that were true, it would appear that Fannie and Freddie preferreds are undervalued based on election probabilities.

Equity Restructuring Considerations

The legal system does not seem to protect shareholder's rights if those shareholders are shareholders in government sponsored enterprises that are regulated under the Housing and Economic Recovery Act of 2008. Hopefully, this doesn't bleed over into the Federal Deposit Insurance Act which regulates the FDIC, but that remains to be seen.

Fannie Mae and Freddie Mac have been retaining earnings since 2019. Treasury has a commitment with Fannie Mae and Freddie Mac that it has neglected since 2021 with respect to submitting plans to Congress on how it intends to restructure its equity position in Fannie and Freddie to enable them to end their conservatorships and attract private third-party capital.

The Congressional Budget Office put together a report in 2020 "Effects of Recapitalizing Fannie Mae and Freddie Mac Through Administrative Actions" where it outlines that the only way to disenfranchise junior preferred shareholders is through receivership. Given the 5 years of retained earnings, receivership is not actionable and so junior preferred shareholders basically are just waiting for the day when the companies undergo the necessary equity restructuring Treasury has promised that will facilitate the ends of their conservatorships. Note that according to this CBO report, additional retained earnings do accrue to help monetize the SPSPA face value in an equity restructuring with a lower earnings multiple.

Summary & Conclusion

In a world where it surely becomes inadvisable to hold the enterprises captive in conservatorship when their net worth eclipses their ERCF capital requirements, and where the Republican Party at large supports the end of conservatorships, my strategy is to continue to accumulate junior preferred at a discount to their intrinsic value. Fannie and Freddie have more net worth than ever before in history and a stronger earnings profile than ever before in history. They are safer than ever before in history. The acting CEO of Fannie Mae indicated that someone doesn't know how to take a victory lap by ending the conservatorships. I couldn't agree more.

I own 15371 FMCCG, 6135 FMCCI, 71767 FMCCJ, 2372 FMCCK, 40019 FMCCM, 12719 FMCCN, 1786 FMCCO, 111323 FMCCS, 615 FMCCT, 2701 FMCKI, 5742 FMCKJ, 1746 FNMAJ, 50 FNMAO, 17682 FNMAS, 21644 FNMFN, 5 FNMFO, 773 FREGP and 100 FREJN. Most of those have been bought since the Supreme Court Collins v. Yellen ruling that drove the prices down which drove me to quit my job to raid my 401k to self-direct ROTH IRA, reprioritize my payment schedule and work two to three times as hard since then to buy as much as I can in anticipation in their eventual release from conservatorship.

Looking back, it was not the Supreme Court Summer 2021 that I thought it was going to be. It was a gift horse of lower prices to buy on a collision course with retained earnings, ensuring that I would get paid soon enough. Come on in, the water's warm! I would file this under one of those things that happens very slowly and then all at once. The current price is remarkable, and that is the purpose of this article.

www.ingramcontent.com/pod-product-compliance
Lightning Source LLC
Chambersburg PA
CBHW071055240526
45469CB00006BD/2309